# Brief
# Encounters

## Edith Newman Devlin

BRIEF ENCOUNTERS
First published 2008
by New Island
2 Brookside
Dundrum Road
Dublin 14

www.newisland.ie

ISBN 978-1-905494-94-1

British Library Cataloguing Data. A CIP catalogue record for this book
is available from the British Library.

Printed in the UK by Cox & Wyman
Book design by Inka Hagen

10 9 8 7 6 5 4 3 2 1

*Brief Encounters* is published in association with
the Bookshop at Queen's.

Bookshop at Queen's
2008

*To all those adventurous people
who travelled with me*

# Contents

# Introduction

When and how did working-class people from the new British industrial cities begin to travel? Until the invention of the railways, ordinary people seldom travelled more than a few miles from where they were born. Trains changed all that. In 1860, the first railway to take passengers as well as heavy goods went from Manchester to Liverpool, soon to be followed by a network of railways which joined one part of Britain to another and unified the country in a new way. People began to think nationally rather than locally – in the face of railway timetables, local time zones had to be done away with, national chains of shops were created and national newspapers were born. The railway was an extraordinary phenomenon which, along with the computer in our own time, was the most important invention for three hundred years. Londoners could now get fresh milk each morning from the country. Tess of the D'Urbervilles brings milk to the railway station to be delivered to London and the elderly Wordsworth went to London by train instead of coach. Railway agencies offered day excursions to the coast and working men could take their families to the sea and get back again that evening. The excitement of going away in a big steam train was part of the drama – all that power thrilled both man and child. And then, to gaze at the limitless sea, to run upon the sand and come home again wearied with sleep and fresh sea air. The ordinary man had begun to travel!

My entry into travel came more than a hundred years later. From my Royal Navy father, I heard of such exotic places as Constantinople, Izmir, the South China Sea, Singapore and South Africa, but I never thought I would have a chance to see any of them. Back then, foreign travel was the exclusive preserve of the rich. But there was another source of adventure. I could travel through books – not travel books, which I did not read, but through nineteenth-century novels. In the novels of the Brontës, Jane Austen, Hardy and George Eliot, the characters seldom travelled far from where they were born. Tess of the D'Urbervilles had never even been in the next valley until she was forced to look for work there. Jane Austen's characters never get much further than Bath or Lyme Regis and George Eliot's characters live within a few miles of a village or a family estate. They live and move in these confined spaces. Their authors know and love these places and make intimate connections between the characters and the landscape. In her beautiful, dignified, vulnerable self, Tess of the D'Urbervilles is an emanation of the rich and fertile valley of the Great Dairies in Wessex, while Catherine in *Wuthering Heights* is a fierce embodiment of wild, savage Yorkshire.

In the late 1970s, I decided to explore this connection and gave a series of talks to voluntary adult students who were interested in great works of literature. These books had a profound effect on them, being a lot more than mere stories. They expanded their horizons and made them think and feel in new ways. Over the next thirty years, we went on to read more and more masterpieces of world literature and to be deeply affected by them.

The Brontë novels figured prominently in my first series of talks. It was impossible not to be overpowered by them. At the end of the course, an idea came to me: why not go to Yorkshire and see the places they so powerfully created in their books? Plenty of my students were willing and eager to go on such an expedition. There were few literary tours then; they were not seen, as they are now, as magnets for tourists and profit. We organised it all ourselves, from the boat to Heysham from Belfast and the coach to Haworth, to the hotel and guide. The moors were indeed bare, wild, windswept and savage. The Brontë parsonage was square, grey and forbidding and the unhygienic cemetery close around it, where all of the children were buried by their father, the Rev. Patrick Brontë, was a sad sight. The museum had not yet been built nor the parsonage done up. The back door was open as if Emily had just slipped out onto the high moor. Charlotte's dress was flung over a sofa in the sitting room as if she were about to come down from the bedroom above to claim it. The clock stood on the landing where, every evening just at nine, on his way to bed, Patrick Brontë wound it up. We sensed the Brontë presence throughout the house. We had lunch at the Black Bull, a pub where Branwell got drunk and from where he had to be carried home. It was a modest, old-fashioned country pub where, after sandwiches and a hearty drink of cider, we fell asleep on the hard wooden benches.

The next year, it was off to Hardy country. No landscape could be as lovingly created as Hardy's Wessex. Rich, verdant, fertile, it is completely different to the harshness of Yorkshire. Hardy's house at Little Bockhampton was not then prepared for mass tourism. The curator was so glad to see such a group as ours that he put himself out to welcome us and show us around. He took us into Hardy's garden, set us down and went to the village himself to buy the makings of ham sandwiches and tea for a picnic in the garden. We felt we were Hardy's special guests. The valley of the Great Dairies where Tess fell in love with Angel Clare seemed unchanged. Huge herds of cows grazed contentedly in the water meadows, though they were now black and white as opposed to brown and white in Hardy's time. We moved to the higher ground of Flintcomb Ash, where Tess and the women pick turnips in the biting cold, work so harsh that only women would do it.

An extraordinary opportunity came along in 1974 when Thompson's Holidays offered the first package holiday behind the Iron Curtain.

# Introduction

Leningrad – city of Dostoevsky, Gogol, Akhmatova, of the terrible Nazi siege which killed a million people – was now open to foreign tourists for five days, all in, for £48 from London. It was not to be missed! The taste once created, our appetite for foreign travel increased. Year by year, we followed Flaubert, Balzac, Tolstoy, Milosz, Gibron and Kadare to see the regions where they lived and wrote. My aim was to see as much of the world as I could before mass tourism and Americanisation changed the old ways forever. I think I succeeded in that just in time. I tried to get to know all I could of the literary and cultural experiences of those countries and in particular to immerse myself in Islam.

What are the conditions for profitable travel? You must leave your preconceptions behind; you must be curious about people; you must be ready to give attention not only to educated people, but to porters, maids and children; you must feel that you are talking not to a foreigner, but to another human being who happens to inhabit another place, climate and culture. Travels like these bring many brief encounters that are still full of human interest. We soon learned that in spite of differences of place, status or culture, we all belonged to what Samuel Johnson called 'the Great Republic of Humanity'. The following pages tell of some of these brief encounters.

# Going Home to Dublin,
## or How to Stop an Express Train
## in the Middle of the Night

*1950*

It had been a tiring journey from Paris to London via Dieppe. I still had to face a five-hour train journey from London to Holyhead, then a four-hour journey by boat to Dun Laoghaire, then on by train to Dublin. I was a student at the Sorbonne going home for Easter. I was to catch the 7 p.m. train from Euston Station to Holyhead. Imagine my surprise and disappointment when we were told that this train was full and we would have to catch the relief train at 10 p.m. instead. There was nothing to be done. People began to queue at the left luggage office to put in their baggage and to be free to roam.

I knew what I would do. I had seen a cinema down the road, so I would pass the time there, whatever the film. I lined up with the others at the left luggage office and scarcely paid any attention to the girl in front of me until she suddenly started to totter and then fell down on the ground beside me. I bent over her – her eyes were open, her face contorted. She seemed to be having some sort of a fit. I asked the man behind me to keep an eye on her while I ran to find the first aid team. By the time I got back, she had recovered, was on her feet and asked me to help her put her luggage in the office. The medical team arrived on the scene and called an ambulance to take her to hospital. I drew a sigh of relief. She would be looked after. I put her left luggage ticket in her pocket and let her go.

I made my way to the cinema and reported back to the station at 9.30, in good time to find a seat on the train. Suddenly, there was an arm on my shoulder. I turned around to see one of the ambulance men. 'Here's your friend. She walked out of hospital this morning in her extreme anxiety to get back to Ireland. She has epilepsy. The doctors have given her drugs which will keep her free of fits until she gets back to Ireland. Just look after her, will you? Keep her warm and quiet.' So the girl, Brigid, was my 'friend' and I was now in charge of her.

Together with our suitcases, we made our way to the front of the train, where there were still some vacant seats. As I walked along the platform, I could see the familiar sights inside the compartments – people huddled up in coats trying to sleep away the five-hour journey, others trying to keep their children quiet. I got Brigid into an empty compartment, helped her to settle herself in a corner by the window and placed myself in the other corner opposite. She looked less pale than she had before. She lit a cigarette and puffed away. She was a maid, she told me, and she didn't like the people she was working for. They gave her too much to do and hardly ever spoke to her. Once back in Ireland, she would stay there even though there was no work to be had. A neighbouring man, unmarried and lonely but twenty years older than herself, wanted to marry her. He was no great catch, but maybe she could do worse. It would be exchanging one form of slavery for another – she knew that only too well – but what else could she do?

Ten o'clock struck. We were off! I shut my eyes and tried to imagine that I would sleep. I heard a noise. I opened my eyes and looked across at Brigid. Her face was contorted and her cigarette slipped from her fingers – she had begun to foam at the mouth and was slipping to the floor. She was having an epileptic fit. I raised her up and tried to remember what I had been told at Guides about epilepsy – put a spoon in the mouth and try to stop the epileptic from swallowing the tongue. I had no spoon. I tried to put my scarf across her tongue. She reacted instantly, kicking and flailing her hands. She slowly grew quiet again and I helped her back onto the seat. She demanded a cigarette. I carefully put one between her lips, but I didn't like the drooping expression of her eyes. I held out a match for her to light it. No sooner had I done so than she began to show symptoms of another fit. I tried to extract the cigarette from between her lips but each time I tried to do so, she grew violent. I had to stop her from burning herself. What was I going to do? The compartment was empty. Just then, I heard the guard come down the train. I appealed to him to help me, for I could see that I might be in for a long night. Yes, he would stay with her while I went down the train and appealed for a doctor or nurse. I got no response from any of the figures engulfed in their coats. Two American men came to help. They offered her brandy from a hip flask, but I felt that brandy wouldn't help her condition and refused it. They went back to their seats and the young guard and I were left alone with our patient.

By this time, one fit was being followed by another. She was purple in the face and quite violent. It took both of us to hold her down or lift her up. She began to try to hit the guard, suspecting him, it seems, of trying to interfere with her as he tried to loosen the blouse around her neck to let her breathe more easily. She wouldn't let him touch her at all. I now had to deal with her myself. She got up, said she wanted to go to the toilet but rushed instead to the compartment door and tried to open it. Here was another awful hazard. 'There's only one thing for it,' I said to the guard. 'You must pull the communication cord and stop the train! She could die here beside us. We must get her to hospital!'

The train wasn't due for its first stop until Crewe, hours away yet. The guard told me that he was only newly a guard and that this was his first night at work! If he pulls the communication cord and stops the train in the middle of nowhere, he'll have to put flares on the line back and front, write reports, etc. and he doesn't want to do it. It's hard to believe, but in 1950 there was no communication possible between guard and driver, no way to have the train stopped. However, he knew another way of dealing with the situation. You could try to communicate with a stationmaster by throwing a stone out onto the platform as we shot past stations with a message tied around it with an elastic band. This message asked for the next signal to be red so that the guard could get down onto the tracks and speak to the driver. He threw a stone out at one station, then another, and the train hurtled on.

By that time, Brigid was very difficult to control. I could feel my legs trembling under me. She might die. At last, at the third station, somebody must have got the message, for some miles further on, the guard saw the signal at red in front of the train. It slowed down and stopped. The guard leapt down and climbed up to the driver's cab. Yes, the train would stop at Cleckheaten and we would get help. As the train got underway again, the noise of children crying could be heard – they'd been woken up by the stopping of the train. Their parents tried to hush them. Brigid's face was purple and her blouse was half torn off from the struggle I was having with her. The cigarette had to be kept ready to put in her mouth, although she couldn't keep her lips pressed upon it. It was a dangerous manoeuvre for me to keep it in place.

The train again slowed down and came to a stop. The door opened and two policemen entered the compartment. An ambulance was waiting to take Brigid to hospital, but she couldn't be moved from the train without the authority of the police. Seeing them, I moved off quickly. My responsibility had come to an end. I heard Brigid screaming and kicking on the floor. The policemen grasped her legs and arms and pulled her to her feet. They carried her off the train and into the night. I fell back into my seat, agitated and exhausted. The young guard was likewise exhausted. He sat down beside me and put his arms around me. We fell asleep together in a warm, thankful embrace.

I never heard anything more of Brigid. It was a brief but memorable encounter.

# Two Irish Girls in Russia

## *1803–1808*

At fourteen years of age I read *War and Peace* and was so overwhelmed by it that from that time I became an enthusiast for everything Russian. Then, in 1973, I was told of the adventures of two Irish girls who went alone to Russia and remained there for some years and left an account of their experience.

It was a dramatic story – sad, even heartbreaking. It was told to me by a friend in Belfast, Arthur Brooke, the direct descendant of the two girls concerned.

It all happened at the beginning of the nineteenth century, when it was most unusual for unmarried girls to travel far from home. Jane Austen's heroines travel no further than Bath or Lyme Regis, but these two Irish sisters, Martha and Catherine Wilmot, got to Russia. Martha stayed there for five years. Each made the long sea journey alone to St Petersburg, Martha in 1803 and Catherine in 1805. It was a huge adventure. They both left behind lively accounts of their experiences in letters and memoirs, some of which have been published. Here was something I could take a great interest in, for I had long been a lover of Russian literature and history. To see Russia through the eyes of two Irish girls like myself would be particularly intriguing. Moreover, their letters were lively and witty and a pleasure to read.

Martha and Catherine Wilmot couldn't have expected to travel further than to their father's relations in England. He had been an army captain in Ireland, then became Port Surveyor of Drogheda, then of Cork. He married Martha Moore, daughter of Reverend Charles Moore of Innishannon, Cork. She came from the nearby Lota House, where she and her parents and siblings regularly made music. Handel was one of their guests. With Captain Wilmot, she settled near Glanmire in Cork. She had three sons and six daughters, all of whom had a musical education. Martha was born in 1775, Catherine in 1773. The girls were cultivated, intelligent and spoke foreign languages. It was an unusual household. The novelist Maria Edgeworth wrote of that time (the late eighteenth century to early nineteenth century), 'In general, formal large dinners and long sittings were the order of the day and night. The fashion for literature had not commenced and people rather shunned than courted the acquaintance of those who were suspected of having literary tastes and talent.'

Then a great chance came Catherine Wilmot's way. In 1801, their neighbours, Lord and Lady Mountcashel, were planning to go on the obligatory Grand Tour of Europe and they invited Catherine to accompany them. Lady Mountcashel was an interesting and unconventional woman. She was not only charming, cultivated and attractive, but she had 'advanced' opinions. In politics she was a republican and in religion a free thinker, having had as governess an even more unusual woman, Mary Wollstonecraft, author of *The Rights of Woman* and mother of Mary Shelley, herself wife of the famous poet Percy Bysshe Shelley. Catherine, vivacious and witty, was an excellent companion and in the two years they all spent in Europe she had many adventures. She dined with Napoleon and his famous minister, Talleyrand, she met the infamous Madame de Stael, General Lafayette, the sculptor David and the famous beauty Madame de Tallien. 'There was something in Madame Tallien's air and appearance that absolutely transfixed me to the spot where she was even before I knew it was she. I was caught by the most entrancing smile I ever saw. She wore no rouge and yet looked fresh and lovely!'

While Catherine was away, her younger brother died in the West Indies of yellow fever. Back at home, Martha was devastated. She sank into such low spirits that her parents were extremely worried about her. The Wilmots had a cousin, Mrs Hamilton, daughter of John Ryder, Archbishop of Tuam. She was concerned about Martha and suggested to her parents that a visit to Russia might help her recover her spirits.

While taking the waters at Spa, Mrs Hamilton had come to know and love a Russian aristocrat,

Princess Dashkov. This princess was an exceptional woman for her time, or indeed any time. She was an intellectual and corresponded with many of the great men and women of Europe, including Voltaire, Marie Antoinette and Frederick the Great. So advanced was her knowledge that she was made the first Director of the Russian Academy of Arts and Sciences, while the Americans made her a member of their prestigious Philosophical Society. She took her son to Edinburgh University to be educated by such men as Robertson and Blair. She had travelled widely and visited Ireland at the invitation of Mrs Hamilton. She crossed from Port Patrick to Donaghadee, visited the Giant's Causeway, 'which is indeed worth a visit', saw Killarney, heard Grattan speak at College Green and stayed in Dublin for nearly a year, where she was received with great warmth by Mrs Hamilton and her friends. Princess Dashkov wrote, 'My stay in Dublin now seems like a happy dream which lasted a whole year. But my enjoyment of it was no illusion for the care and affection of my friends, Mrs Hamilton and Mrs Morgan, the attention and respect of their families anticipated my every wish and made my days flow in peace and contentment ... In the evenings we went out. Dublin society was distinguished by its elegance and wit, its manners and was enlivened by that famous frankness which comes naturally to the Irish.'

The princess visited the Wilmots in Cork and invited them all to visit her in Russia, after which she returned home. Some years passed. Then, in 1803, Mrs Hamilton persuaded Martha's father to allow her to accept the princess's invitation. Martha had always wanted to travel and her sunken spirits were revived at the prospect. In the spring of 1803, she set out alone, her father making sure she was escorted in Dublin and London.

At Yarmouth, it was six days before the ship could even get underway. 'The journal of my life may be comprised in three words – squalmish, squeamish, sick,' Martha wrote. After seven days of sailing, she at last saw St Petersburg at three in the morning. 'I saw the sun rise in splendour over the shining spires and domes of this great city.' The princess, whose estate lay sixty miles south of Moscow, had arranged for her to be met and entertained in St Petersburg. 'They guessed my age to be nineteen [she was twenty-six] and told me I was pretty. So they concluded that either I was crossed in love, or my parents wished me to marry someone I do not like or sent me on this voyage to dissipate my chagrin!' Because of her connection with the princess, she was presented at court to Tsar Alexander I and Empress Elizabeth. 'He is a tall, fair, handsomish-looking man – she tall, fair, and would be very pretty only for a dreadful scurvy she has on her face!'

From St Petersburg, Martha made the six-day journey by carriage to Moscow and on to Troitskoe, the princess's estate, sixty miles further south. Martha was immediately embraced in warmth and tenderness by the princess, who was an eccentric indifferent to conventional opinion. 'Her dress, a man's nightcap and black hat with a sort of *robe de chambre* ... This place is splendid. Her English taste presides and she has really created from rather a barren situation one of the most lovely and magnificent places that is to be found anywhere!' Martha's sister left this account of the princess: 'In the midst of this immense establishment and in the centre of riches and honours, to see the Princess go out and take a walk, an old brown great coat and a silk handkerchief about her neck worn to rags and her dress as well may be worn to rags for she has worn it for eighteen years and will continue to wear it as long as she lives because it belonged to her friend Mrs Hamilton ... She helps the masons to build walls, she assists with her own hands in making the roads, she feeds the cows, she composes music, she writes for the press, she talks out loud in the church and corrects the priest if he is not devout ... she is a doctor, an apothecary, a surgeon, a ferrier, a carpenter, a magistrate, a lawyer ...'

At that stage in her life, the princess was extremely isolated. Although she had been famous and fêted in her youth, she was now forgotten. She had helped the Empress Catherine in her coup to secure the throne, and when Paul came to the throne in 1796, he punished those who had worked against him; this included the princess. There were also strained relations with her family.

Martha provided her with a new and rare companionship – loyal, loving, intelligent, cultivated yet unworldly. The two women were drawn into an intimacy which was profound on both sides. The princess showered Martha with presents and made sure she got to know Russian life.

Martha's letters home were full of interest. She describes a party: 'Many a bad dinner have I made from the mere fatigue of being offered fifty or sixty different dishes by servants who come one after the other and flourish ready-carved fish, flesh, fowl, vegetables, fruits, soups of fish etc. etc. before your eyes, wines, liqueurs etc. etc. in their turn ... Many a time have I wished the wasted food of their fatiguing feasts transported to little Erin which too often wants what is here despised. Certainly gaiety is not a characteristic of this country. On the contrary, their music, their dance, their countenances all have a tendency to the penseroso: and take them all in all they are extremely handsome. I speak only of the lower orders, as for the higher, I decidedly prefer our islanders. The same principle seems to pervade all – servility.'

She describes her day: 'I rise at half-past seven, breakfast and coffee in my own room which is a most cheerful and agreeable and well-furnished apartment. At eleven or twelve I visit the Princess and we chat, sometimes about Kings and Empresses and sometimes about wheat or rye for half an hour or so. I then return to my own room and dress, or not, just as I like etc. etc. I read the Psalms every day as such a thing as a Protestant church is not known here, and at two we dine, our dinner superb and well-dressed with cleanliness and delicacy. From dinner we retire to the drawing room till four and then out to walk in the beautiful grounds of Troitskoe'.

Several years passed and Martha's parents became anxious for her return. Her sister, Catherine, had by then returned from the Grand Tour of Europe and their father suggested that Catherine should travel to Russia, visit the princess and bring Martha home. So Catherine made the long sea journey to St Petersburg accompanied by her Cork maid, Eleanor Cavanagh. Martha was overjoyed to see her sister after such a long separation. 'My precious Kate is arrived! O my God, excessive joy is a painful thing.' The princess extended the same warm welcome to Catherine as to her sister. She loved both girls devotedly, but it was Martha who was her favourite. Catherine's letters home are lively and witty and she comments very intelligently on Russian life: 'Russia is still in the fourteenth and fifteenth centuries.' To the lively maid from Cork, this country was exotic indeed.

She writes home with all the drama, gaiety and verbal spice of a native Irish woman: ''Twas two days after we went that we quit Mr Booker and sail'd 8 miles across to a fine Palace. God knows I wou'dnt know the name off it, wou'dnt be Orangeenbaum! There another Coach & 2 Servants with ugly beards (one of them as red as a Rose) came to take us 30 miles on to Petersburg! Why, wou'd you believe it, ma'am, they put 4 long-tail'd Horses all in a row & then 2 again at the end of long rope traces (& they seldom cuts the Manes of them at all, for down they hang in bushels of plaits, or else without them)! And Ough! My God! To hear the Smack & the Cry that the Postillions give, & how they drive like Smoke up the Hills! That I mightent! But I made full sure to myself that we were fairly out of Ireland then! I never see anywhere in Glanmire such a shew of Places and big Woods as them all by the Country at either side while we drove along ... I'll never forget how beautiful Petersburg look'd the first day. Cork is a flay to it & the River as large as the Lee 5 times over: I don't believe they call it by that name tho! We slept that Night at Mr Raikes in a great Church of a House; very civil People, & all as one as Mr Read or Mr Anderson down at Fermoy! They gave me plenty of Convaniences to wash out the things we dirtied in the Ship, & indeed the Soap too was good enough. I'll engage I got Tai & fine Craim (& plenty of it) for my breakfast, & Miss Raike's Maid give me a nice border of a lace Cap & Miss Wilmot's white wrapper dress'd me up smart enough to go with the Servants of the House down to see the Palace. I thought the Screech wou'd have Choak'd me when turning round my head what wou'd I see leaping over a rail Rock but a Giant of a Man on the back of a Dragin of a Horse. 'Stop him' (sais I), for I declare to God,

Miss Henrietta, but I thought the Life wou'd have left me to see a live Christian making such a Fool of himself, when what did I hear but that he was a Marble Emperor! Some old Snake of a Man that they call Peter, or Pater the Great, or something like that!'

The princess was now so emotionally dependent on Martha that although her parents urged her to return, she couldn't bring herself to leave 'my Russian mother'. In 1807, Catherine sailed for Ireland without her sister. Martha might have stayed in Russia forever had war not broken out between England and France, after which her presence aroused suspicion, with some saying she might be a spy. Further, the princess's daughter was jealous of the presents and attention spent on this unknown Irish girl. Information was laid against her. Martha was deeply disturbed by this turn of events and her departure became imperative. She took a heartbreaking leave of the princess and made the journey from Troitskoe to St Petersburg, where she attempted to negotiate her passage on board a frigate. When she learned that the captain was to sail without his wife and daughters, she thought it would not be proper for her to sail with him alone.

On hearing that the princess was ill, Martha was struck to the heart. She turned and made the long six-day journey back to Troitskoe. 'At two o'clock yesterday I arrived and were it possible to feel perfect happiness in these cruel, cruel times I ought to do so in the unfeigned affection of my best beloved Princess and that of every creature in the house. The Princess flew to meet me at the hall door and burst into a flood of tears. She folded me in her maternal arms with an ecstasy that was almost painful. I was as much affected as she was … My departure had been regretted as the death of a person dearer to her than anything on earth.'

But Martha eventually had to leave the princess for good. The princess's attachment to the two sisters led to their being accused by the princess's enemies of trying to supplant her own children, not only in her affections, but also in their inheritance. The sisters were even watched by government spies. In 1808, Martha was obliged to say farewell to the princess, knowing that she would never see her again. Soon after Martha left, the princess became ill and died, 'having nothing left to live for'. 'How all is changed at Troitskoe: the theatre is closed, I have not had a single performance; the pianoforte continues silent; the *femmes de chambre* have ceased to sing. Everything paints your absence and my sorrow.' Fortunately, though, Martha had earlier prevailed upon the princess to write her memoirs, which have been preserved and published.

Martha was deeply affected and wore black for a year to honour the princess's memory. She later married the Rev. William Bradford of Storrington, Sussex, who became chaplain to the British Embassy in Vienna. Martha finished her life with her daughter in Taney House, Dundrum, Dublin, where she died, aged ninety-eight. Catherine Wilmot never married. Soon after her return from Russia, she was found to have TB and was advised to move out of Ireland to a drier climate. She moved to Moulins in France, where she remained for four years with only a few visits to England and Ireland during that time. When her health deteriorated, she moved to Paris, where, after a few weeks of great pain, she died in 1824, aged fifty-one.

I was very moved by the stories of these two courageous and intelligent Irish women. I made a vow to myself: I would visit Russia and try to get to Troitskoe. I didn't know how, though, for the Iron Curtain had descended firmly on Europe. It seemed like a pipe dream. But it happened!

# Leningrad
## *1974*

Leningrad, city of the great Dostoevsky and Pushkin, city of the terrible 900-day siege by the German army in World War II, and now firmly behind the Iron Curtain. It was the winter of 1974. We had been reading Pushkin, Gogol, Dostoevsky and Solzhenitsyn in the comfort of our homes. The Cold War between the USSR and the rest of the world was at its height. The Berlin Wall between the West and communist East Germany seemed set for decades to come. The Iron Curtain was firmly in place all over Europe. Then something quite unexpected happened. Thompson's Holidays advertised a five-day package holiday to Leningrad from London, all in, for £48! It was so cheap because it took place in the cold of February. We didn't hesitate. A group of us signed up, even taking some of our children out of school for 'educational' purposes. Our visas weren't issued until the last minute – a special way the paranoid Soviets had of keeping a continuous watch on you. One of our party, although packed and ready to go, was refused a visa, no reason given. Her enraged husband flew to London to demand the visa from the Soviet Embassy, but was also refused.

The lady deduced the reason for the refusal: her husband was the manager of Belfast Airport – she might be on a spying mission for him!

Stocked with woolly hats, scarves, gloves and boots, we set out. The bus commissioned to take us from Heathrow to Gatwick failed to arrive. We were in shock! Another was eventually hired, which started out two hours late. It seemed certain that we would miss our Aeroflot flight, though a phone call to Gatwick from an AA box got us a promise that the plane would wait for such a large group. On arrival, one hour late, we were rushed straight onto the plane, where our excuses were met by hostile expressions from the Russian hostesses and cheerful patience from the British passengers. We settled down to enjoy our three-hour flight. We saw Copenhagen below us in the darkness and we began our descent towards Leningrad and the mysterious Soviet Union. The hostesses came down the aisle and demanded our newspapers and magazines. No news of the outside world must reach the eyes of a Soviet citizen. It was our first taste of a police state.

We landed safely on Russian soil on the other side of the Iron Curtain. As I reached the open door of the hatch at the top of the gangway, the cold air cut like a knife. Before me, on either side of the gangway, I saw soldiers drawn up in two lines in grey uniforms and fur hats, rifles in hand. Was this a welcoming party or a stern warning? (British air crews weren't allowed to leave their

plane and they had to make a quick turnaround.)
We passed down the gangway and into the airport
terminus, wondering what was going to follow.

We had to form a long queue at passport control. An expressionless official (the Russian face
had learned this through hard experience) seated
behind a no doubt bullet-proof glass motioned to
us to hand over our passports. He turned the pages
very slowly and deliberately, stared long and hard
at a console hidden from our eyes by a high shelf,
stared at us again – impassive, almost sinister –
again at the passport, again at the console. I felt
like a prisoner in the dock. A curt motion of the
hand and I was through.

On the journey from the airport to the city, we
could make out little in the dark save large lumps
of dirty snow on the side of the road, an odd light
from a high apartment block, then the dimly lit
streets of Leningrad itself. There was nobody
about, although it was only ten o'clock at night. We
drew up outside our hotel, which was large and
drab in what we came to know as the typical Soviet
style. Receptionists were unsmiling, almost hostile.
It may well have been their first encounter with
'rich' Western tourists and they weren't going to
be impressed. We made our way to our designated
floor, where we were met by another Soviet phenomenon – the *dezhurnaya*, or key lady. She was a
formidable, squat woman who controlled not only
the keys of the rooms, but the comings and goings
of the guests and no doubt reported everything to

an official. My room was sparsely furnished, with no curtains on the windows. I fell into an exhausted sleep on my first night in Russia.

The next morning, the light pouring in through my window awakened me. I rushed to the window to see Russia outside! All the drabness of the day before was quite forgotten in the brilliance of what I saw. The hotel faced the broad expanse of the River Neva. I saw an intensity of light before me, pale, diaphanous, almost ethereal, such a light as can only be seen in the northern countries of Europe, light so luminous that it was impossible to tell where land ended and sky began. Only a long, low line of buildings told me of the city nearby. A long, slender, elegant spire of pure gold rose shimmering in that light – it was the spire of the Peter and Paul Fortress. Soon, my eyes, grown accustomed to the brilliance, could make out large blocks of ice floating down the water. Not far from my window, the battleship *Aurora* was anchored, whose guns had given the signal for the Bolshevik Revolution to begin. It looked beautiful against the blue and white of the Naval Cadets' College, where a line of cadets in smart uniforms were drawn up to perform some morning ceremony. I made a quick descent at the appointed hour, for I was certain that some sort of punishment would follow should I fail to appear on time. The meal was set out in a huge Soviet-dimension dining room, where our places were designated

and were not to be changed. Breakfast was bleak —
a spoon of damson jam in a glass of water serving
as juice, raw eggs, a stale roll and weak coffee. I
tried out my Russian on the waiter and got no response. My neighbour, a Pole, whispered, 'Don't
let them see you know Russian. They will take you
for a spy!'

We gathered in the hotel foyer to wait for our
Russian guide. This was a moment I had been
looking forward to for years — to seeing the beautiful, famous, notorious city of Leningrad (St Petersburg was renamed Leningrad after Lenin's
death in 1924) I had read about in Russian literature. This was the city whose heroic resistance to
a ferocious siege by the German army in the Second World War gripped the imagination of the
world. In its rapid advance into Russia in 1941, the
German army reached the environs of this city
and set up house in the magnificent Ekaterina
Palace, where they looted and destroyed the precious objets d'art and stripped its walls of their
amber. They were determined to take their time
before smashing the last defences of the city, to
terrorise and starve its inhabitants into submission.
Hitler was so inebriated by the certainty of his victory that he issued invitations to a victory party to
take place at the city's famous Astoria Hotel. Yet
against all the odds, the city held out. The siege
lasted 500 days, and in that terrible time, nearly 1
million people died of starvation, disease and cold.
They dropped dead in the streets and ate cats and

dogs and rats to stay alive. For its resistance, the Soviets designated it Hero City.

Thus it was fitting that our first visit that first morning should be to the Piskaryovka War Memorial, where thousands of Leningraders are buried in mass graves. It was bitterly cold in those great green acres. A statue of Mother Russia stood at one end, while on the other, an eternal flame burned. A guard of honour stood to attention, rigid and unmoving in the glacial air. 'Nobody is forgotten. Nothing is forgotten,' reads the inscription. There were few people about. Newlyweds arrived in black saloon cars for the bride to lay her bouquet in tribute to the city's dead. Respect for the dead of the Great Patriotic War is intense all over the Soviet Union. In subsequent visits, we saw guards of honour at war memorials in every city and every small town of schoolchildren who replaced each other with solemn ceremony every fifteen minutes. More people were killed in the USSR in the Second World War than anywhere else in Europe.

We were taken on a city tour that morning. In the winter sun, the pastel blues, greens and ochres of the buildings combined with the pale azures of the sky to make this a city of pure poetry. As we gazed in admiration at the exquisite harmony of building, water and sky, we almost forgot the price paid for the creation of such a city. In the early eighteenth century, Tsar Peter the Great thought of founding a city on the water facing Europe, a 'window on the West' to rival Paris and Rome and be a port for commerce far removed from Moscow, the 'Asiatic' heart of Russia. Peasant serfs were drafted in to drain this swamp and divert its water into canals. It was a pestilent site and perhaps 1 million serfs died during its construction. They are buried in the inhospitable islands of the Neva Delta. Architects were brought in from all over Europe to design public buildings and private palaces and in 1712, Peter made the city his capital. Under succeeding tsars, it became a cosmopolitan city with a splendid royal court and a large trading centre. From here, autocratic tsars ruled Russia for a further two hundred years, until their downfall at the hands of the Bolsheviks in 1917. The Bolsheviks, fearing a German attack on the city, moved the capital from Petersburg to Moscow in 1918. It is still contentious as to whether Moscow or Petersburg is the real heart of the Empire. Stalin feared Petersburg as a rival power to himself in Moscow and had one of its leaders, Kirov, assassinated. (He is quoted as saying, 'One man, one problem. No man, no problem.')

In the evening, we were told we were 'free' to walk about the city ourselves. This was a surprise, as we knew how paranoid the authorities were about allowing foreigners free rein. We soon saw that the fear was indeed real. As we gathered in the foyer of the hotel to go out and explore the town, we saw a woman rise from a seat and follow us out. She was a most obvious spy. She followed us at a short distance, turned when we turned, never letting us out of her sight. The children found this to be the most interesting episode of their whole visit. How exciting to be followed by a spy! They ducked and dived in and out of shrubbery and doors to see if she would follow. She did! This happened every evening, and as there were many groups in the hotel other than ourselves, an army of spies must have been employed. There was distrust and suspicion everywhere. Ordinary Russians trudging along the street averted their eyes from us foreigners. Waiters, guides and curators were certainly under instructions to keep their distance. Talking to foreigners carried heavy penalties. No Russian was allowed into our hotel. A bouncer kept the door and inspected our residents' cards. We understood that he made money by accepting bribes from those who wished to enter illegally. Discreet offers of tights and cigarettes were eagerly accepted. Young men furtively offered to buy our clothing – jeans, trainers, jerseys, anything. Had we dollars or sterling? They would give us Russian roubles in exchange. As there was nothing to buy, roubles were useless to us. The few objects on offer for sale to foreigners were to be found in special shops and all money had to be paid in dollars.

The drabness of the people was in stark contrast to the beauty of the buildings. Although it was February and both cold and damp, boots were made of synthetic material, headscarves did duty for fur hats and heads were kept down, taciturn and impassive. The famous department store, the Dvor, was practically deserted. Where once chic clothes from all over Europe were sold, now only a few garments of poor quality were displayed. Row after row of display stands stood forlorn and empty. When goods did come in, they were sold 'under the counter' on the black market by the assistants. Queues formed wherever food appeared for sale. I saw the eternal patience and endurance of the Russian people on the faces of the women in the queues. On the wide main street, the Nevsky Prospect, there were hardly any cars and only one or two small 'cafés' where you had to stand to swallow a cup at speed. There was no concept of leisure in this city, first battered by German armies and then by its own government. Gigantic pictures of Lenin looked down from hoardings on the inattentive, passive people on the streets. 'Learn, live and work according to Lenin,' they commanded. Other gigantic hoardings displayed pictures of the new 'heroes' of the Soviet Union, men and women who had achieved huge production figures. That year was the thirtieth anniversary of the lifting of the siege of Leningrad: flags were flying from every public building and pictures displayed the heroism of the Soviet citizen, heroes pictured in clean, positive, energetic poses, marching chin forward into the future. In contrast to the West, there was no piped music, no near-pornographic film displays. The USSR was, on the surface at least, strictly puritan.

I asked a guide about the possibility of attending an Orthodox service. She didn't know of any, she said. Taxi drivers proclaimed the same ignorance. The Soviet system was solidly atheist. To prove the point, we were taken to the famous Kazan Cathedral, now designated the Museum of Atheism, where we were shown how so-called 'miracles' were manufactured. We watched the tears of the Virgin stream down her beautiful face and were then shown a machine behind her head which manufactured these tears. Russians, although not absolutely prohibited from practising their religion, knew that such practice would do them harm in their job and in other areas of their lives. We did find a functioning church, the ornate church of St Nicholas. Various services were going on at the same time; the body of a young girl lay under a white gauze shroud in an open coffin, waiting for the burial service, while several baptisms were being performed alongside her. The few people in the church were all ill-clad old women. There was none of that colour and joy we were to experience in Orthodox churches after glasnost. We wandered through the cemetery of the church of Alexander Nevsky, where many famous musicians are buried. We came upon three women weeping bitterly over a grave. They were mourning their bishop, who had died some three weeks earlier: when allowed to express emotion, Russians readily do so.

For us, St Petersburg was the city of famous writers. There were many literary house-museums open, but many others that weren't, for obvious reasons, until after glasnost. We knew that Alexander Pushkin's apartment was open as a museum. Pushkin is the most famous Russian writer and the most beloved by Russians, beloved in a way that's hard for us to understand. It is a deep love, far exceeding the lip service paid to Shakespeare in England and to James Joyce and Beckett in Ireland – bus drivers can quote his poems and schoolchildren recite them. He was a great poet and storyteller. He was the first great Russian writer (of the time of Wordsworth and the English Romantics) to compose his works in the Russian language, a language considered at that time to be the language of peasants, whereas French was the language of the educated and which is spoken in Tolstoy's novels. Pushkin's novel in verse, *Evgeny Onegin*, set to music by Tchaikovsky as an opera, is known wherever opera is loved.

His own life was as extravagant as any opera. As a member of the nobility, he received a good education. He wrote poetry from an early age, including witty epigrams against the tsar and against autocracy, for which he was exiled to the Caucasus. Although his punishment was light, his life was in real danger when it was learned that he had been one of the group of intellectuals known as The Decembrists, who planned a coup against the tsar in 1825. The group was caught and its members sentenced to death or exile. Pushkin got off because he was not actually in Petersburg at the time of the coup. Nevertheless, he took the precaution of burning his papers. From that time on, he was watched by government spies and his verses were constantly censored, as a free mind was anathema to the tsar.

The ebullient and witty poet continued to write poetry and was later exiled to his mother's estate in northern Russia. We made the long journey to visit this estate, in green, lovely countryside, where he listened to his old nurse tell stories of old Russian ways and Russian folk tales. It was there that he wrote *Evgeny Onegin*. Having looked over the homely house, we went to the church in the cemetery where his body was buried. As is the lovely custom in Russia, we laid roses on the grave as a tribute to his genius.

Pushkin fell passionately in love with a beautiful but penniless young girl, Natasha. They married and had four children. Natasha was so admired for her exquisite beauty that in order to have her constantly at court, the tsar had Pushkin made a gentleman of the bedchamber, thus requiring his frequent presence at court. This was a humiliating position for a man of Pushkin's birth and genius. In addition, he was required to see Natasha surrounded and admired by other men whom he despised and who despised poetry. A young French army officer, d'Anthès, an émigré from the French Revolution, pursued Natasha relentlessly. It is said that he even married her sister in order to be near her. Anonymous letters began to circulate in Petersburg calling Pushkin a cuckold. The passionate and jealous Pushkin, envenomed by these insults, challenged d'Anthès to a duel, which took place in a field near the city in March 1837. Pushkin was mortally wounded and died two days later. He was thirty-seven years old. His death caused a sensation in Petersburg and the police, fearing a popular rising, had his body taken away for burial during the dead of night. No honours were accorded him. (Many other famous writers in Russia were also buried hurriedly to avoid public demonstrations.) His body was transported by ordinary sledge to a monastery near his country estate in the north of Russia.

D'Anthès was expelled from Russia after the duel. He returned to France, married and lived a long, prosperous life. The tsar had advised Pushkin on his deathbed to 'die like a Christian' and promised to provide for his wife and children, which he amply did. After seven years, Natasha remarried, this time to a Russian army officer.

So edgy was the Intourist guide that she wasn't willing to take us to see Pushkin's apartment in the city, so we found it for ourselves on the Moika Canal. The woman curator greeted our group with unfeigned enthusiasm. Had we indeed heard of Pushkin in Ireland? Did we know his poems? In Russian? Alas, by reading them in translation we had missed everything, for his poetry was 'pure champagne'! Then she relived the last two days of his life for us – here was the bed on which his wounded body was placed when he was carried from the field of the duel, here the stairs where his devoted friends thronged to hear bulletins of the state of his health, outside was the street where hundreds of his followers waited for news (her own devotion was clear). Here is the desk on which he wrote many of his poems, poems, she said, which will live on as long as men do. We emerged from his apartment on the Moika Canal much moved by what we had seen and heard.

# Mr John's French Adventure

*1975*

A comic interlude occurred during a visit to Normandy. A group of students were accompanied by a professor of history, a professor of geography and myself as commentator on Balzac, Flaubert and Proust, all associated with this province. Mr Stephen John always sat in the front row. He was always in position when I came in, large, portly, wearing a dark suit, shirt and tie, very correct, a man of about seventy-five looking as if he had spent all his life working in the civil service. It was the first year I had offered to conduct an extra-mural class in the university, a class open to anyone interested in the subject and with no obligation to sit exams or work for diplomas. That year, there were fifty-six subscribers. Class followed class and the numbers grew. Mr John joined every year and never missed a session. He always came in early and always sat in the front row, where he could see people enter from a side door. The subject that first session, in 1968 to 1969, was Love and the Woman Novelist. This was a subject I was investigating for myself in those years before feminism in literature had become a major industry. Among the novels I had chosen were George

Eliot's *Middlemarch*, Charlotte Brontë's *Jane Eyre*, Edna O'Brien's *The Country Girls* and D.H. Lawrence's *Women in Love*.

This new topic excited comment. As he was drilling my teeth, my dentist asked, 'Are you the woman who is teaching the Dirty Books Class?'

'Are you, by any chance,' I retorted when I could, 'mixing up love and sex?' I don't think he understood the distinction.

A lecturer in science called out to me, 'My wife wouldn't be seen dead in a class like that!' Education of a certain sort was needed in puritan Belfast.

Mr John never missed a class. Was he, too, expecting me to unveil the secrets of sex from a woman's angle? He made one or two very prudish comments, rearing up, so to speak, at any implication that love between men and women could be anything other than noble, beautiful and Presbyterian. I asked him one day why he always sat in the front row. 'From there, I can watch the ladies come in and admire their outfits,' he replied.

Every year, I took a group from the class to places connected with certain writers. We had visited Brontë country, Hardy's Dorset and Pushkin's St Petersburg. Mr John told me how much he wanted to be one of the party, but his wife, an invalid, couldn't be left alone. His children were all resident in England, so he had nobody to call on. He would have to be satisfied with the books. One year, we came to Flaubert and Balzac. Why not go to Normandy and Brittany, to places connected with these two writers? We could take in the famous Norman castles in the company of Professor Lewis Warren, historian of the Normans, and Dr Robin Glasscock, specialist in the geography of the area. I would cover the writers. It would be a rare cultural experience. At the mention of Normandy, Mr John got very excited. Normandy! For years, he had longed to see those great Norman castles! There was nothing else half so interesting! He would consult his daughter and see what could be done. How could he possibly miss such an opportunity! To my amazement, he arranged the whole thing. His daughter would come from England and look after her mother for a week. It was March. I warned Mr John that it could be very cold and those castles freezing.

'I never catch cold,' he exclaimed firmly.

We set off, Mr John encased in a long great coat. He was very correct, very aware of his own dignity in this exceptional situation, surrounded by many stylish, laughing women. On the second day, the invulnerable Mr John caught a cold. Very intemperately, he had taken off his great coat. We spent that night in a small, comfortable hotel. In my capacity as tour leader, I gave Mr John two aspirins and advised him to go to bed. He who never caught cold would be better in the morning. After dinner, I knocked on Mr John's door. A muffled 'Come in' came from inside. I opened the door cautiously.

'I came to see how you were, Mr John.'

'Not good. Not good.'

I ventured to put my hand on his forehead. It was very hot and wet. He must have a temperature. I risked pushing back the bedclothes a little bit to see if he was in a perspiration all over. He immediately pulled them back up again, this time right under his chin. But I had felt his pyjama top – it was soaked right through. Little as I wished for any intimate contact with Mr John, I determined to be valiant.

'I'm afraid I'll have to change your pyjamas, Mr John. They are wringing wet. Have you another pair?'

His horror was palpable. Change his pyjamas! What exactly were my intentions? He drew the bedclothes tight under his chin. I rummaged in his suitcase and found another pair. Here my courage failed me. I could not, even on the point of death, change the bottom half of his pyjamas. Looking as if he were going to the scaffold, he finally slackened his hand and let go the bedclothes and I hoisted him up in the bed. He was heavy, inert, and I could barely manage him. I drew off his pyjama top, washed him down as quickly as I could, dried him, put on the dry top and let him slip back under the sheets. He was perturbed.

'If you aren't better tomorrow, I'll send for the doctor,' I said. 'I'll look in before midnight and give you two more aspirin. Goodnight, Mr John.'

I went straight to my room to recover my

composure. Midnight came. I knocked again at Mr John's door. No reply. My goodness, was he dead? I opened the door softly. His eyes were open and he looked at me strangely.

'How are you? Are you still perspiring?' I asked.

No answer.

'Mr John, I'll have to see if your pyjamas are wet. I've felt your forehead and I don't think you have a temperature, but you can't lie in wet pyjamas all night.'

Mr John said nothing. He still had that strange look about him, an excited air, you might say. Suddenly, with a dramatic movement of both hands, he pulled the bedclothes right off himself and lay there, exposed, and said in a strange tone of voice, 'Here I am! Do what you like with me! I am yours!'

What could he be thinking of? Surely not...! Abruptly, I pulled the bedclothes back over his exposed body and gasped, 'No need for that. No need for that at all. I've dried your other pyjama top and will change that. Nothing else. You'll have to lie in your wet pyjama legs until morning.'

He quivered again as my fingers sponged down his ample chest and back. It was all I could do to complete the job, for I was suffering from shock. I tucked him up, said I would look in during the night and withdrew. He never took his eyes off me. At two in the morning, when I looked in, he was fast asleep. I didn't enquire about the state of his pyjamas.

The next morning, I called the doctor. Standing next to him beside Mr John's bed, I suddenly felt more resolute and courageous.

'You did the right thing, *ma chère*,' said the doctor. 'You have brought down his temperature. To-morrow, when you are all due to leave, Mr John can go with you, well wrapped up. He has a strong constitution.' Yes, I thought to myself, *very* strong!

The next day, Mr John got dressed and we all boarded the bus. Two sisters-in-law, both very attractive, one blonde, one brunette, said that they would help look after Mr John. They took turns sitting beside him, cheering him up, laughing, enquiring about his comfort. He went from one to the other in a delirium of joy! He didn't even look out the window. He paid no attention to the Norman castles he had so much wanted to see. He had got something much better.

# Turkey: Sailing to Byzantium

## *1978*

One of the great names of history is Constantinople, or Byzantium, the meeting place of Europe and Asia. It has been home for over a thousand years to Hagia Sophia, the greatest church in Christendom and the site of gorgeous mosques and palaces, now all neglected and run down.

It was the spring of 1978. Two friends, art historians, announced that they intended to visit Turkey for a period of three weeks. 'Why go there?' I asked, amazed.

'Art of a very high order,' they replied. 'Byzantine and Turkish art. We don't know what the conditions will be, probably dreadful, as Turkey is in a very bad way economically, but what we shall see will more than make up for any discomforts.'

This was something new. I had never thought of Turkey as an interesting destination and I had never heard of Byzantine art. If I thought of Turkey at all, it was of a primitive place with bad roads, a bad climate, poor food, disease, unfamiliar religion, mosques and minarets. Did this instinctive indifference go back to what we had been told at school about the Crusades and those 'chivalrous' Christian knights who had bravely fought the infidels? How much of it was Christian propaganda? Then, too, I knew that Turkey had been on the 'wrong' side in the First World War. Everything about that country seemed unattractive.

A week in Istanbul in the spring of 1978 changed all these ignorant preconceptions. I discovered that Turkey was one of the most interesting countries in the world. Over the next twenty-five years, I visited all of Anatolia (the name for the Turkish homeland, or Asia Minor, which is what the Romans called this province of the Empire) except for the extreme south-east, where a running battle between Kurdish rebels and Turkish forces still goes on.

The problem for the visitor to Turkey is seeing all that there is to see. Apart from the exquisite beaches and high mountains which draw thousands from all over Europe, Turkey is one big archaeological site. Such a rich country, placed as it is between Europe and Asia, has drawn invader after invader to its land. Fourteen known civilisations have, at one time or another, occupied it and have left beautiful, intriguing remains behind them. Troy, the site of the greatest battle known to man through the pages of the *Iliad*, is in north-west Turkey, and Homer, its author, was born in Turkey, as was Herodotus. Greeks from the mainland colonised the Aegean coast of Turkey from 600 BC and built such splendid cities as Pergamon, Ephesus, Miletus, Didyma and Priene. Abraham, in the Bronze Age, lived in Harran in south Turkey. The site of the biblical flood is said to be in east Turkey on the plain underneath Mount Ararat, where Noah's Ark is said to have come to rest. Ephesus is where St Paul, in the theatre, decried pagan customs and enraged the silversmiths who made a living from idols. Antioch is where St Peter hid away from the fury of the Jews of Jerusalem after the Crucifixion, and St John is said to have brought the mother of Jesus to live with him near Ephesus after the Crucifixion and is said to have written his Gospel there. Turkey is also home to the seven churches St Paul visited on his missionary journeys. The great early heresies in Christianity originated in Turkey and that mysterious relation between the Father, Son and Holy Spirit was bitterly disputed there. Heresies were declared and schisms created. Finally, the Nicene Creed, which fixed the main tenets of Christianity for centuries, was promulgated in Nicaea.

The Turks like to be appreciated for themselves and for the extraordinary, rich culture they have created. Istanbul, not Constantinople, is the name of their city. Yet it is their Byzantine past which brings the curious traveller to its shores. The Byzantine Empire was the name of the eastern part of the Roman Empire, as distinct from the western part, with its capital at Rome. The eastern part separated from the western in the early fourth century and survived long after the Empire had crumbled in the west. The Byzantine Empire flourished for many centuries until, in the thirteenth century, wave after wave of Turkish tribes, fleeing before the Mongols, broke into Asia Minor from the east. They gradually colonised almost the whole of Anatolia and slowly but surely weakened the Empire. Over time, they got closer and closer to Constantinople, the heart of the Empire. By 1453, the Turkish tribes called the Ottomans held the city in a vice. Sea and land walls protected the city and a great chain had been stretched across the piece of water called the Golden Horn to prevent the Ottomans from moving their ships up the Horn and hence nearer the city. The siege of the city lasted seven weeks. The Turks had their boats pulled over land and into the Golden Horn. The Christian people of the city, terrified, crowded into Hagia Sophia to pray for deliverance from the Infidel. The final Orthodox liturgy in the famous church took place shortly before sunset on Monday, 28 May 1453. Throughout the night, everyone prayed fervently for a last-minute salvation. The Emperor paid a final visit to the church just before midnight in order to make his peace with God, then repaired to his post on the battlements. Shortly after sunrise, word came that the defence walls had been breached and the city had fallen. The people inside the church barred the great door and awaited their fate, trembling with fear. In a short time, men of the vanguard of the Ottoman army forced their way into the church, slaughtered those who resisted and led the rest into bondage. The long and brilliant history of the Byzantines had come to an end.

My first impression of Istanbul in 1977 was of a broken-down, shabby city. Pavements were cracked and broken and the big commercial warehouses along the Golden Horn, where once big ships unloaded their precious cargoes, was in a very bad state of repair. The waters were dirty and scum-covered and gave off a sour smell. Half-starved dogs roamed the streets, covered in filth and lice (these were later all shot as a matter of hygiene). The shops in the main streets were poorly stocked and uninviting. Little 'pudding shops' offered cheap but good food and stayed open late. There were few good hotels and none served alcohol. But nothing – not all the dirt and shabbiness – could obscure the magnificence of the city and its position, set on seven hills overlooking the waters of the Sea of Marmara, the Bosphorus and the Golden Horn.

Istanbul straddles two continents, Europe on the north side and Asia on the south. All day long, busy ferries clanked and hooted as they crossed the water from one side to the other, bringing people to and from work. From the water, the skyline of the city is one of the finest in the world. Ship ride at anchor under the city walls and large ships continually pass up and down the

Bosphorus on their way to and from the Black Sea.

We were overpowered by the Bazaar, lost among its many labyrinthine streets, with its shops full of gold bracelets, earrings, jewels, rugs, suitcases, leather goods, spices and dried fruit. Down by the water's edge at the Galata Bridge, a pulsating mass of humanity bought, sold, fished, ate, smoked, talked, gossiped and did business. The Roman Hippodrome, centre of Byzantine life with its seat for the Emperor, where races were held and membership of a team was a political statement, was (incredibly) still there. Right beside it was the great church we all wanted to see, Hagia Sophia, the most famous building in Turkey.

Its great square bulk sits solidly beneath its dome, all pale ochre pink, quite unlike any Western church. Inside, the enormous dome seems to float unanchored in space, unsupported by pillars. Justinian had employed celebrated physicists to work out how to do this. When he entered his great creation for the first time, he exclaimed, 'Glory be to God that I have been judged worthy of such a work! Oh, Solomon, I have outdone you!' Even now, shorn of its church decorations, its icons, lamps, candles and overlaid by huge Islamic writings on the walls, it is overwhelmingly impressive. When the Greek liturgy was celebrated here, myriad small lamps lit the interior, candles blazed before the icons and the vestments of the priests, while the chanting of the choir made the space seem like paradise on earth. The precious marble and porphyry which cover the walls echo each other's intricate veins from wall to wall. The huge mosaic of the Virgin with the Child in her lap in the apse is still radiant, commanding and calm. Most of the other mosaics were plastered over by the Muslims, partly to protect them and partly because Islam forbids the making of human images in sacred art. These mosaics were later restored. It was strange to think of the famous people who, long before us, had come here to stare and wonder, Tamburlaine among them.

Damage was done to the great church, including earthquake damage, but the most scandalous damage of all was done not by the Muslims who preserved it, but by other Christians. The Turks aren't barbarians – they respect Christian saints. The Christian crusaders in 1203 determined to sack the city. Since the ninth century, there had been an increasing estrangement between the two great Sees of Rome and Constantinople, which eventually led to an open and lasting schism in 1054, a breach that has not yet been healed. The two are not in communion with each other. The crusaders, having taken the city, sacked it and the violence and brutality of their actions shocked witnesses on both sides. They looted and pillaged monasteries and convents and set up Roman Catholic rule in the Orthodox Church, a rule which lasted sixty years and scandalised the Orthodox.

Our hotel, The Park, was unassuming but comfortable and, with the better-known Pera Palas Hotel, it was, during the First World War, a centre for spies of many nations. I wondered if, during this present Cold War, it still served the same purpose? Nearby was a café where, after our busy days, we ate the most delectable cakes you could find anywhere.

The Istanbul Opera was near our hotel. It had a full company and a full repertoire in spite of Turkey's dire economic situation. As we were passing, the stage door opened and a large, young Turkish man emerged, together with three or four companions. Spotting us as tourists, he hailed us in English. 'Welcome to Turkey! Where are you from?' He introduced himself with some pomposity as the tenor soloist of the opera company and his companions as members of the chorus. 'You are from Ireland? Good, good! I know of your famous tenor, John McCormack. He is much appreciated here. How long are you staying in Istanbul? Please, ladies, let me show you our city! It is worth a visit! Have you taken a boat journey up the Bosphorus? No? Not yet? Let me give you a rendezvous for tomorrow at the ferry terminal. I will escort you myself!' He was large, bearded, chest forward, eyes confident, sure of himself. He was soon in expansive mood. 'Lady, look at me! I have everything in the world I could want. I am at the top of my career. I have a house and yes, I have a car, but I lack something to make my life complete.'

'What is that?' I asked, intrigued.

'A wife,' he said. 'I do not want a Turkish wife, for Turkish women are not educated. I must have an educated partner who can understand and appreciate me as an artist. A French woman, now, or even an English woman!' We laughed to ourselves.

'I have a daughter at home,' I ventured merrily. 'She's eighteen years old, speaks French and Spanish, is handsome and plays the cello.' His eyes lit up. 'Lady, she would do exactly for me! If we marry, I would not expect her to live in Turkey. We will live in Paris, Milan. I will be good and respectful to her and I will be most respectful to my esteemed grandmother-in-law!' The gaff was hilarious. I did not correct him.

'According to the Koran, how many camels must you give me for my daughter?' I asked, laughing. 'Forty? One hundred and forty?' So I bantered, but he was serious. That day, I sold my daughter for one hundred and forty camels!

The next day, we arrived at the ferry terminal at the appointed hour. Our tenor arrived soon after with his four companions. He descended on us with lavish greetings and embraces. We were hustled onto the already crowded ferry. It was Sunday and a holiday. 'The captains of these ferries know me and respect me. They will invite me and my party onto the bridge and away from the crowds.' And so it was. We were led up stairways to the bridge. The whistle gave a snort, the holding

chains clanked, the engine revved and the ferry
drew away from the dock. 'My Irish friends, shall
I give you a solo?' With that, our tenor opened his
mouth and burst into an aria from *Carmen*. His
voice was full and powerful. The crowds on the
lower decks grew hushed as his voice carried down
to them. When he finished, they burst into ap-
plause. Again and again he sang. We were so en-
chanted, we scarcely took in our historic
surroundings as the ferry crossed from side to side
of the Bosphorus. We came ashore at Sariyet near
the top end, for the very top where the Bosphorus
enters the Black Sea is a forbidden military zone.
Our tenor guided us and his friends to a very good
fish restaurant. We ate and talked and laughed and
when the bill was presented we hardly noticed that
we were paying not only for ourselves, but for our
tenor and his four friends as well.

When we reluctantly came to leave the restaurant, we found that the last ferry had gone. Our
tenor suggested hiring a boat and soon he had se-
cured one and we all went aboard. As the boat got
underway, darkness descended and the moon rose
over the waters. The romance of our situation
struck us all. We floated along blissfully for some
miles. Suddenly there was a stir, a muffled shout.
One of our party had fallen into the water and
she couldn't swim! The boat made a sudden turn
to avoid Vera being caught in the propeller. By the
time I got down to the lower deck, one of the
valiant members of the chorus had dived into the

water and had caught Vera, still clutching her handbag and believing that no one had seen her fall and that she was about to go under forever. The drenched Vera was hauled aboard and every one of us took off our jackets and wrapped her, shocked and frozen, in them. She had caught her heel on a stair and had been rocketed forward and through a gap in the railing of the deck and straight into the Bosphorus. That gap should not have been there and the owner of the boat was very worried in case we lodged a complaint against him. We were now all struck with horror at the thought of what could have happened.

I asked for us to be put ashore at the nearest point to our hotel, rather than going on to the terminal. As we mounted the steep hill to the hotel, shots rang out quite close to us. Here was an unforeseen and added danger. Turkey was in a state of anarchy, its economy failing, and terrorists and rebels were making regular warfare against the state police and army. We had seen the tanks and soldiers massed outside all banks and important buildings, but we hadn't yet seen any actual fighting. Atila, our guide, took charge as usual, leading us up a side street and into our hotel by a back way. We were all relieved to be safe at last. We gave Vera a hot bath and called the doctor. What if Vera caught pneumonia? I had been told that her husband doted upon her and everyone was surprised that he had let her go on holiday without him. The thought of having to face Gordon was appalling. The doctor arrived, examined Vera and declared her to be suffering from no more than shock. The magic of the day had now completely evaporated.

The next morning, Vera was up for breakfast as usual and made little of her misadventure. I wouldn't have to face Gordon after all! Nevertheless, I wrote to him when I got home. The next year, both their names were down to go with me to Crete. Was he, the doting husband, going to keep his eye on her? I was sure of it. I was wrong. He turned out to be a charming, good-humoured and gregarious Welshman and a delight to us all. As we sat under a warm sun in Xania in Crete, Gordon turned to us five women. He leaned forward and said with great charm, 'I would marry each one of you were I not married already!' Under the spell of Crete, we partly believed him.

# Nemrut Dağ

*1979*

After eight or nine hours of driving in temperatures over ninety degrees Fahrenheit, we were tired when we pulled up outside the Banana Hotel in Adiyaman. We were now in the deep south-east of Turkey and the transition from the civilised west of Turkey to this landscape of high, barren mountains, remote villages and intense heat was like moving to another continent.

Why had we made this long journey? To see an amazing sight – the huge ceremonial tomb on top of a very high mountain of a man who thought himself a god. Even before the Romans invaded this land they were to call Asia Minor, even before the birth of Christ, a local king, Antiochus I Epiphanes, had immense delusions of grandeur. His father, Mithridates I, had prided himself on his royal ancestry, tracing his forbears back to Darius, king of Persia, to the east and to Seleucus, Alexander's general and founder of the Seleucid Empire, to the west. His son Antiochus was an astute ruler and he grew rich. He became so puffed up that he saw himself as equal to the gods, reasoning thus: Alexander the Great had conquered this kingdom. Alexander was regarded as a god and Antiochus was his descendant; therefore, he, too, was a god. To demonstrate this equality, he had a funerary mound built for himself on a nearby mountain, Nemrut Dağ, over six thousand feet high. He employed an army of slaves to haul up huge stones to construct it. This fantastic monument lay undetected for centuries, hidden away in the clouds. Only in 1881 did a German engineer come upon it as he was prospecting the area for possible transport routes for the Ottoman Empire. Investigation into the complex only began in 1953. By the time of our visit in 1979, it had seen very few tourists indeed; we were again pioneers.

It was eleven o'clock at night when we reached Adiyaman. As usual, Atila took command. Our reservations had been made weeks before. We were glad to let Atila do all the work, work which he always did well. He was deep in conversation in Turkish with the owner behind the simple reception desk, a conversation which seemed to go on for much too long. Atila never lost control or showed anger, so we were mystified by the delay.

Presently, a young boy about ten years old appeared. He looked alert and quick and his eyes shone with intelligence, as do the eyes of many Turkish children. The owner spoke to him in Turkish, took some money out of a drawer and put it into his hand. The boy flew up the dim stairway. He reappeared with a look of triumph on his face and put a key down on the desk in front of the owner. Atila stood by, wooden faced. Again the operation was performed, again the same result. Atila turned to the group and announced the numbers of five rooms and the names of the people who were to occupy them. The rest of us waited, puzzled. At least the older members had now got a room and a shower. But had they?

Soon we heard steps coming back down the narrow stairs and into the lobby. 'There are a man's trousers in my bed! There are crusts of bread between my sheets! There is men's clothing in my wardrobe!' More consultation followed between the now angry Atila and the owner.

'Madame, these will all be cleared away! Give me ten minutes, please!' Meanwhile, the sending of the boy and the delivery of the keys continued. 'Your rooms are ready now, ladies. Please take your keys!' We were all exhausted and impatient by this time. But before we could mount the stairs, down came some of our group. 'Our sheets are dirty! They haven't been changed! We would rather sleep on the bus!' Smiling, patient, ready to solve all problems, the owner gave further orders to the boy, who again disappeared up the stairs.

It was now clear to us what had happened. Late at night, the owner, thinking that our group was not going to honour our reservation, had let out our rooms to some Turkish men. When we arrived so late and so unexpectedly, the Turkish men had been woken up, assailed by the servants and offered money to vacate their rooms in a great hurry and to go onto the flat roof to sleep under the stars. They had had to vacate their rooms, leaving their trousers and supper behind them. We waited a further thirty minutes. 'All sheets have been changed. You can go to your rooms,' the owner said with an encouraging smile. As I waited, the last, for my key, three or four exasperated people reappeared in the lobby. 'Our sheets are soaking wet!' They had just been washed! Remonstrations began again between Atila and the owner, who brought these difficulties to a final and beautiful conclusion with the words, 'In this climate, ladies, sheets dry very quickly!' We had come to the end of our possibilities. We retired to our rooms, so tired now that we hardly cared where we slept. We had no sooner turned off the light and settled ourselves when we heard the handles of the door being turned. Here was another 'circumstance'. We got up, barricaded the doors with chairs and suitcases and were soon back in bed and fast asleep.

The next morning had been appointed as a pre-dawn rise, for dawn was known to be the best time to see the tumulus on top of Nemrut Dağ. Indefatigable travellers as we were, we accepted a change to a nine o'clock departure and less dramatic view of the mountain. We breakfasted in a small room off the foyer, a surprisingly good breakfast of tea, eggs, yoghurt and excellent Turkish bread. The rooftop Turks breakfasted alongside us, smiling, and seemed to bear us no ill will. Only people who are used to comfort complain.

We were to travel by coach to the foot of the mountain and then onward in jeeps. The drivers were Kurds, for this was Kurdish territory where, in 1979, Turkish law did not rule. My driver was a big Kurd with a handlebar moustache and a gun. We were distributed among the four jeeps and my Kurd ceremoniously signalled to me to get in beside him in the front. As everyone knows, these four-wheel drives have a multiplicity of gears and my driver changed gears excessively, for each time he did so, he ran his arm up my leg and side! I leaned away from him. He leaned closer and took advantage of every jolt in the road to fall over on me! The others in the back seat saw what was happening and giggled openly. This man had a rifle and was not to be trifled with. Atila, my possible saviour, was in one of the other jeeps.

After about two hours of driving, we had a break at a broken-down little tea house where the children stared at us, wondering why so many women would travel up the mountain to see a heap of stones at the top. The hair of the poor little waifs had ginger streaks, a sure sign of malnutrition. I was determined to get into the back seat for the rest of the journey. 'I have had enough massage. One of you can take my place,' I said and jumped into the back. A commanding voice then said, 'Not in back, Madame! In front!' and in front I had to get, the others overcome with laughter in the back.

We climbed further and further up the mountain until we came to a rough platform, where I jumped out. We walked the last few hundred yards, until suddenly we saw in front of us, right at the top of this mountain, an amazing sight – the remains of huge temples and terraces and colossal stone men seated in a row, like men from outer space who had just landed in their space suits. But they had lost their heads, which lay about in the debris, two metres high – Hercules, Zeus, Apollo and Antiochus himself among his perceived equals. We looked into their bland, unseeing eyes, at the aristocratic disdain on their beautifully modelled heads and headgear and at the inscription in Greek: 'I, Antiochus, created this monument in commemoration of my glory and that of the gods!' It was a breathtaking assertion. It's said that an earthquake toppled the heads, but I believe it was Poseidon, the earth-shaker, who sent the earthquake to punish Antiochus for this show of hubris. A second terrace balanced the first and a core of earth and rocks was piled up between them. Perhaps Antiochus himself is buried beneath it? It hasn't been excavated. We wandered over the broken, grandiose place among the remains of incense altars, monumental stairways and terraces. These gods had looked out over the elements for over two thousand years and here we had come to intrude on them. It seemed almost sacrilegious. I though of Shelley's 'Ozymandias':

> *My name is Ozymandias, King of Kings.*
> *Look on my works, ye mighty, and despair!*

*Nothing besides remains. Round the decay*
*Of that colossal wreck, boundless and bare*
*The lone and level sands stretch far away.*

My Kurdish driver was lying in wait for me at
every corner of the site. 'This way antiquities, lady!
Follow me, lady!' I declined his invitations. We had
a picnic on those airy, heavenly terraces and never
had we eaten in such a fantastic setting. We
climbed back into our jeeps for the journey down
the mountain. This time I avoided the driver, and
he had given up on me. It was a steep and wonderful ride. We stopped on the banks of a fast-
flowing river to admire a Roman hump-backed
bridge. Although exhilarated by our experience, we
were now hot and tired. What about a dip in those
cool waters? Who had a bathing suit with them?
Although unlikely, there were certain wise virgins
among us who always had oil in their lamps and I
was one of them. We raced each other into the
water. How cool and lovely it was! We laughed and
splashed and felt like gods ourselves. A slight
movement by the side of a pillar of the bridge
made me look up. A young man was kneeling in
prayer, his face rigidly turned away from us, no
doubt towards Mecca. He could no longer resist!
He turned around and saw us meagrely clad foreign women splashing in the water. A look of horror came over his face and he fled.

# Trebizond
## *1979*

We arrived quite late in the evening in this famous town and learned that some five or six of us couldn't be accommodated in our hotel. No need to worry! Accommodation could be found elsewhere! We were taken to a rather shabby, small hotel on the main street and into a large room, scantily furnished with five or six beds. Against one wall of the room was a sort of elevated throne on a large concrete stand. This turned out to be our communal toilet! We laughed as we chose our beds and promised each other that we would close our eyes when one of the five was on the 'throne'.

We slept well and woke refreshed. Suddenly, we heard the sound of a brass band. We looked out our window and saw the whole band walking erect down the main street. They were all wearing smart red and black uniforms, their instruments gleaming. What were they celebrating in such style in run-down, poverty-stricken Turkey? Was it a Muslim holiday? A trade union congress? We didn't know, but the sight of that band in its orderly march, its brilliant colours and its stirring music was an ironic contrast to our room and our 'throne' and ourselves. These two images return every now and again to my mind.

Rose Macaulay's *The Towers of Trebizond* has given the world a romantic image of this old town on the coast of the Black Sea. Its days of glory are over, but the old church of St Sophia on a plateau above the sea reminds us of that rich past. We paid a visit to Ataturk's lovely old villa, now a museum, where we looked at memorabilia of that extraordinary man.

As we passed along a small street in the town, we saw through an open door of a small shop five or six girls busy on Singer sewing machines embroidering placemats. They looked up and smiled. We went in and asked them about their work. Yes, they worked long hours, but they enjoyed each other's company and were glad to have a job. We came from Ireland? The look on their faces was blank. I drew two circles, one big, one small, close to each other. 'This big one is England; this small one is Ireland.'

'Very small?'

'Yes, very small.'

'Smaller than Turkey?'

'Yes, much smaller.'

'Do you like Turkey?'

'Yes, very much.' As we turned to go, I asked Tosun, our guide, 'How shall we wish these lovely girls well?'

'*Kolay gelsin!*' he said. 'May your work be easy!'

We waved goodbye, saying, '*Kolay gelsin!*' They smiled, delighted. We felt warmed by this innocent exchange of friendship.

# Singing in the Orchard in Turkey

*1979*

We left the Black Sea and Trebizond behind and began the day-long journey over the mountains to Erzurum in the east. We knew that the Zigana Pass through these mountains was a hair-raising 6,500 feet high, very beautiful and almost empty of tourists. The slight mist on the coast soon gave way to clear, dry mountain air which acted like a tonic on us. We climbed higher and higher through sinuous valleys and cool, dark pine forests whose perfume filled our nostrils. We noticed a change in the character of the houses in these villages, different from those on the coast. Here, the little houses had flat roofs on which the fruits of the earth were laid out to dry in the sun. Now and again, we passed a man and woman, he riding on a donkey, she walking beside him. Our feminist instincts were roused!

We stopped in the high mountains to stretch our legs. We walked about in the cool mountain air, which was filled with the scent of wild flowers and herbs. We thought we heard the sound of singing coming from nearby woods. It came closer and we recognised the voices of women singing some Turkish folk song. We listened, charmed. Six or seven young women emerged from the trees, still singing. They were about seventeen or eighteen years old, were all dressed in white and wore white headscarves. They saw us, stopped their song and smiled. We clapped and smiled. They came towards us, their outstretched hands full of apples which they had been gathering in the orchard as they sang. They presented a perfect picture of joyful innocence. We must all take apples, armfuls of them, every one of us. They invited us into the orchard, where we could view the trees and help ourselves to yet more apples. They tried out their English on us. 'Where are you from? Do you like Turkey?' They were all students at a high school in Trebizond and would soon be returning for the start of term.

'What will you do when you have finished school?' I asked, curious.

'We will get married, have children, work in the fields and in the house.'

'Will you not have a profession, be a teacher, perhaps?'

'We might do that, but when we marry, we will have to give that up.' I knew only too well the life of drudgery which faced women in rural Turkey. Yet still they were singing.

I thought of Wordsworth and the highland lass singing in the field as she cut the grain:

> *I listened, motionless and still*
> *And as I mounted up the hill*
> *The music in my heart I bore*
> *Long after it was heard no more.*

# Armenia and Armenians

*1979*

We knew of the alleged genocide of the Armenians by the Turks in 1915, a genocide still hotly disputed by the Turks. Armenia is a rocky, mountainous little kingdom which bred highly intelligent and artistic people and where one of the most ancient Christian churches had its beginning.

I was a student at the Sorbonne in 1951 when I met Ara. He was from a wealthy family in Istanbul and was presently a student at the prestigious École d'Administration in Paris. We became friends. He felt that there was something that drew us together in a strange way, he being a child of persecuted Armenians and I being a 'persecuted' Irish woman. That I did not feel such seemed to make no difference to his perception. He was tall and good-looking, but there seemed to hang about his face such an expression of brooding melancholy that I became convinced it must be a characteristic of his entire race.

We talked for hours on end, strolling, sitting in cafés or in the park – we talked of art, philosophy, religion, the meaning of life. I learned for the first time of the massacre of the Armenians – over one million of them – by Turks in 1915, including his grandparents. He found my general Christian optimism touchingly innocent. I knew so little of life there in my out-of-the-way island off the coast of Europe. He was right. I knew next to nothing. He proposed to show me something of the seamy side of life in Paris, to enlarge my absurdly romantic view of humanity. Would I be up to it? Would I go with him to a cabaret in Pigalle, the well-known haunt of Parisian prostitutes? I trusted him completely. Yes, I would accept. Why not? I was not, I assured myself, 'a fugitive and cloistered virtue'. I wanted to educate myself in the ways of the world.

He called for me at the appointed time and we set out in the Metro for Pigalle, mentor and student together. We entered the restaurant by a long, narrow passageway and came out into a dimly lit dining area where our table had been reserved. Never having been in such a discreet restaurant before, I tried to look as if I was quite used to my chair being held for me and to sophisticated menus to choose from. As I relaxed, I began to look around the room and began to notice its clients and its furnishings more closely. I was shocked to see that the table at which we were dining was in fact a coffin. The other tables resembled coffins, too. I looked at the 'pictures' on the walls. Some of them were glass boxes containing the remains of unborn babies. Ara saw me stare and grow red, then white. He pointed to the waiters and waitresses. Underneath their aprons, they were wearing monks' and nuns' clothing. My whole mind in shock, I tried to sit still and appear calm. Ara was watching me closely. Would I be able to take it? I knew I must hold my ground, sit still, be served, eat. I must put on a pretence of the sophistication I was far from feeling. These were 'sick' people, who came to have their least worthy sensation titillated in this morbid fashion. I was sure that nothing like this went on in Ireland. It was Paris. Had my father not warned me? 'Remember, my child, Paris is not Dublin.' I was just beginning to see this. Those little babies in bottles around the walls appalled me. I had never seen an unborn baby, and the very notion of a little half-formed human being in a bottle shown to grown men and women made me sick inside. I could hardly eat anything.

The meal over, worse was to come. The waiters and waitresses now appeared among us in their 'religious' clothing. They were on offer to the guests for sexual pleasure upstairs. One had but to choose. At this point, I could bear it no longer. I rose, found my coat and went with Ara down the passageway we had come in. Had I seen 'life'? Ara assured me that what I had seen was nothing compared to what went on – bestiality, for instance. I implored him to tell me no more – I didn't want to know. He agreed. Could I maintain my romantic, high-minded innocence in the face of this? Yes, I could, I said. Yes, I would.

Ara and I remained friends until I returned to Ireland. I was firm: our friendship must remain platonic. His sad, brooding face has haunted me ever since. One day, I promised myself, if ever I got the chance (it seemed impossibly remote in 1951), I would go to his homeland and see for myself the Armenia which had suffered so much and in which his grandparents had been murdered. We corresponded, sent photographs, but gradually our communication decreased until it finally ceased altogether. Recently, after fifty years, I learned that he was the director of a large bank in Istanbul.

Against all the odds, that opportunity came in 1979. Having had a taste of western Turkey, we were determined to travel east and see that poor but extraordinarily interesting part where even western Turks didn't want to go. It was, in fact, like another land. Where western Turkey was Mediterranean, fertile and Western-looking, eastern Turkey was a wedge lodged in the heart of Asia, bordering Iraq, Syria and Iran. Far from being a Mediterranean climate, it was very hot in summer and intensely cold in winter, so cold that the houses are half-built into the earth to protect them. Here lived the poorest of the poor in poor Turkey.

From Diyarbakir, we made a long, hot journey through the Bitlis Gorge to Van. Van was the ancient capital of the Urartians, ancestors of the Armenians. Lake Van's soft, pale as glass, opaque green, almost soapy water gave off a bodiless, thin light in a wild, flat landscape. The lake was formed when a volcano erupted and blocked the outlet of a river's drainage system. We went by boat to the island in the lake to see the ruined Armenian cathedral of Aktamar. We rapidly changed into our bathing suits and flung ourselves into these cooling waters. Without any warning, we soon found ourselves surrounded by young Turkish men who swam beside and underneath us, hoping to get a glimpse of something prohibited to them, a woman's half-naked body. We must have fed their eyes abundantly that morning!

On our way from Van to Agri, our next night's stop, we passed many poor villages where people struggled to make a living in a harsh, flat, bleak landscape. Naturally, there were no public toilets in such a tourist-free region, and Atila, our guide, had to find something for the women of the group. He found a kind of military barracks, very dirty and ill-kept, where he obtained permission for us to use the toilets. They were extremely uninviting, but we had no other choice. As we women passed through the dark entrance door, a resounding slap on the bottom was delivered from unseen hands.

The small town of Agri, meaning Ararat, sits right under that lone, magnificent mountain. Rising as it does from the plain, it reaches a height of 516 metres and is snow covered even in summer. I had stayed at many dirty hotels in Turkey, but Agri had the distinction of being the dirtiest of them all. (Turkey was not then, as it is now, equipped with first-class tourist hotels.) My bedclothes were so suspicious that I took them all off and laid newspapers and my raincoat on the mattress. I threw the filthy floor mat out on the landing. That night, as I lay down on my improvised bedding, I thought I heard the handle of the door being tried. I got up and silently opened the door. Right along the corridor, outside every door, a Turk was kneeling, his eye glued to the keyhole! I barricaded my door and returned to bed. At breakfast the next morning, no women were visible. All waiting at table was done by men, as was usual in Turkey. These young men were untrained. This was the year 1979, a year of near anarchy in Turkey. Electricity cuts were frequent and water came on and off occasionally. As there was no way of knowing whether your tap was on or off, leaving your room meant risking a flood on your return. One of our group, a very academic and correct Englishman, came back to find his room in just such a flood. Like Stanley in Africa, he squared up unflinchingly to the situation. He shut his door and emerged about an hour later in shirt, tie and suit, perfectly dressed as if for the London scene.

Kars was our next destination, our stepping-off point for a visit to Ani, the famous deserted kingdom of the Armenian people who had once lived and thrived there. The short, sharp syllable of the name Kars itself well expresses its character of a fortress town fortified by the Byzantines on its vulnerable eastern frontier to withstand the on-slaught of the Turkish tribes who attempted to break through from the Asian steppe. I looked up at the grim fortress and wondered how the soldiers stationed there over the centuries had borne the fierce cold, the wind and the monotony of this endless existence. The town of Kars was in such a strategic position that it was besieged and taken again and again by invading armies, including that of the famous destroyer, Tamburlaine. What butchery had taken place in these frozen killing fields, what rape of helpless women? Now the waters had closed over the past and the castle looked down upon us, harsh and unyielding. It was surprising to see so many fine Russian houses in Kars; Russia had seized and occupied Kars in 1878 and had controlled it until 1920. Not even Russians, used to the snow and cold, could have wanted to be sent to this godforsaken outpost.

The Armenia we were about to visit was empty of Armenians. It is alleged that 1.5 million were killed by the Turkish army in 1915. We knew that the wound still festered and we would be careful as to how we questioned Atila, our Turkish guide. Some members of the group were bold – they asked him for the truth of the matter. He denied that there had been a genocide. 'They were a fifth column in our midst. When we were fighting the Russians in the First World War, they collaborated with them in an attempt to defeat the Turkish army and set up an independent Armenia. They killed as many Turks as Turks killed them.' From that moment on, the formerly loyal subjects of the Sultan were viewed as traitors. We knew the similar scenario from living in Northern Ireland. We, too, were sometimes judged to be complicit in the treachery of the IRA or UDA. We knew by Atila's increasingly irritated tone that we had better leave this subject alone.

We needed a military permit to enter the deserted Ani, for it bordered directly on the Soviet Union and Soviet Armenia. While we were waiting for Atila to get this permit, we got out of the bus to look around. Immediately, a crowd of children surrounded us, shouting, 'Pen! Pen!' We went to our handbags to fetch the biros which we had brought with us for this very purpose. The driver of the bus put up his hand in warning: 'Please! Please! Do not make beggars of our children. Children! Go into the fields and gather wild flowers for our guests!' And off they went. Mortified by this just rebuke, we put our biros back in our bags and eventually took them back to Ireland. I encountered such innate courtesy everywhere in Turkey.

Atila returned with our permit. He said we were to take no photos, use no binoculars, make no notes and use no pens, for that might be construed by the Soviets as making maps for military purposes. Once inside the military zone, we looked up at the Soviet watchtowers some hundred yards from us. Soldiers were clearly visible, rifles in hand. I had an instant urge to wave merrily at them, but wisely desisted.

All around us was an awesome sight, a huge, exposed plateau which was once the city of Ani, 'Ani of the thousand and one churches'. Ani Cathedral has been ironically called the finest ruined medieval church in the Middle East. Ani was once a thriving Armenian city on the Silk Route, bustling with merchants, nobles, priests and people – some say one hundred thousand of them – but was now an empty expanse where wrecks of great stone buildings seemed adrift on an ocean of undulating grass, whipped up by the ever-present wind. Broken-down, crumbling walls which had once been a formidable protection for the city, withstanding fierce snow and rainstorms, now gaped helplessly outward to what was once the source of danger – two steep gorges and a river. We walked from one ruined church to another in a strange and haunted emptiness. The churches look small from the outside, but go inside and you will be amazed to find yourself in a soaring cathedral. Armenians love height in churches, and here they have perfected the shape. We found our way into the ruined cathedral, once home to the Armenian Orthodox patriarch. The eye went up and up and where the great dome should have been was a hole in the sky. The dome fell down centuries ago. I closed my eyes and imagined the ghostly procession of patriarch, splendid vestments, mitres, priests and acolytes, incense rising from the censers, the lovely chanting of the Armenian liturgy by the choir, the magnificent icons, the people crossing themselves and bowing low to the ground in devotion and supplication to their God.

Rising lone and majestic from the plain was the mountain of Ararat, holy to all Armenians. Its two peaks, Little Ararat and Big Ararat, are the cones of extinct volcanoes that are snow covered all year round. Many believe that Ararat is the site of the biblical flood where Noah's Ark came to rest. In fact, archaeologists agree that there is extra-biblical evidence of a flood at the relevant time and one man who escaped it. Many people have claimed to have seen the framework of a large boat at the top. Expeditions still regularly go forward to try to penetrate this mystery. For the Armenians, there is no doubt that this is their Holy Mountain, as set out in the Bible.

But although we were there in Armenia, admiring its monuments and its Holy Mountain, there were no Armenians living there – Armenia was empty of Armenians. (The Turks called them Eastern Turks.) Where had those who escaped the Turkish massacre gone? Many emigrated to where their intelligence was given free rein – to the US and to many European countries. But many fled to the other side of the Holy Mountain, where they were protected by the USSR. It was obvious that if we wanted to meet Armenians, we must go to Soviet Armenia, and in a very roundabout way at that, as the border between the two countries was closely sealed. But we had made up our minds.

# The Other Half of Armenia

## *1979*

We had to go a long way round to see the other 'half' of Armenia. Although only on the other side of Mount Ararat in Turkey, Soviet paranoia dictated that we fly to Moscow, from there to Tbilisi in Georgia and from there by bus across the mountains to Soviet Armenia. We had seen the Soviet watchtowers along the Turkish border. We were told that the fields along the border were ploughed up every night so that footsteps could be detected in the morning. This gave a new dimension to 'securing your border'! We crossed briefly in and out of Azerbaijan and had a conversation with two Azerbaijanis at a rest stop. They felt bitter, persecuted and shut in by hostile neighbours, including Armenians and Iranians. These Caucasian Republics have a tough fight on their hands to preserve and promote their independence.

We arrived in a high, barren landscape, wild and unpeopled, it seemed. We came to the famous lake, which I had first read about in Osip Mandelstam's *Journey to Armenia*. Baikal was the world's deepest lake and I had looked into it in Siberia. Now here was one of the world's highest lakes, 1.25 miles above sea level. It seemed as if no one had ever lived there, ever fished in it, ever made a living in this landscape, so we were very surprised when we drew up at a hotel and were taken into the dining room for lunch. What could a hotel be doing here in this unpopulated place? We were even more surprised to be greeted by a live orchestra, summoned hastily in Soviet style, to play for us, the sole diners, during lunch!

Our walk by the side of that huge lake was unforgettable. The surface of the water was a unique green and blue, pure translucency, its waters reflecting the huge expanse of sky above and changing subtly with every light wind. 'Every evening, at five o'clock precisely, the waters suddenly fizzed up as if a huge dose of soda water had been flung into them,' noted Mandelstam.

There was so much to see, such as the prehistoric remains of forts and early monasteries and churches which revealed themselves when Soviet hydroelectric schemes caused the level of the water to drop. But we had no time. Yerevan, capital of this doughty kingdom, awaited! The most startling sight was not the town, the hotel nor the inhabitants, but an awesome mountain which rose up, snow covered, lone and majestic, in the plain. It was Mount Ararat. These Soviet Armenians (taken over in 1920) have never been able to see the Turkish side of their Holy Mountain, for the Soviets won't let them cross the border. We produce photographs taken on the Turkish side of the mountain, the sacred side they have never seen. They fall upon them, scrutinise them again and again, hold them up to the light and then pronounce with great solemnity, 'Our side is more beautiful!' They are full of melancholy. 'My mother and all the family except me were killed in Mus. Our whole race was wiped out by the Turks.' They had hardly got over this 1915 genocide of 1.5 million of their people (a figure hotly disputed by the Turks) when they suffered the Soviet invasion of 1920.

Here we are in Echmiadzin, the theological capital, the Vatican, so to speak, of the Supreme Catholics of Armenian Orthodoxy – and it's Palm Sunday. There are crowds gathering to see the procession of bishops and theological students enter the church. There are forty students training for the priesthood in the monastery, hope in atheistic Soviet Union. The Soviets turn a blind eye, as Armenia is very important in their scheme of things. The people are educated and highly industrious. They make precision instruments for the Union in exchange for energy and raw materials.

We are caught up in the general excitement. Besides, this is all new to us, we don't know what an Armenian service is like – Armenians, the first nation to embrace Christianity! A long line of black-clad figures, silver cross on breast and wearing huge black headdresses, cross from the monastery to the cathedral. The crowds press into the church after them. Our guides, who are having a hard time keeping an eye on us, tell us that it's forbidden to go into the cathedral. We go in. Tanya catches up with me. 'Who is this virgin Mary they talk about?' She knows nothing of the Christian story in atheist Russia. My neighbour at the mass whispers, 'You must go out of the church backward so as not to turn your back on God.'

How have the Armenians held so tightly to their national identity over so many invading centuries? Their strong Christian belief is one reason; another is their attachment to their history, to legend and fairy tales. They start with the children. They do something very striking: they educate their imagination, that part of the personality that makes experience 'real' in a way that the academic does not. Children are taught stories and legends and myths, are encouraged to paint and draw and construct, and are even allowed to do this on the city's footpaths. It's the only country in the world, after the USA, which has a museum of children's art, the only country I know which has a fine opera house entirely run by children who write, direct and act and charge to go in! The museum was brilliantly alive with primitive paintings, masks and collage expressing the legends of their country. Although they prize books and education above all else, they know the supreme value of the imagination. Every child is taught a musical instrument. The country has produced many musicians, including the famous composer Khachaturian, who thoroughly researched the country's folk art.

The pagan and Christian live side by side in Armenia. Echmiadzin's cathedral is built on a pagan site. At Gegherd monastery, I saw an altar outside the church wall where a priest was sacrificing chickens.

We were to be at Yerevan Airport at 6 a.m. to catch our flight to Moscow. We arrived on time. The early rise was worth the effort when we saw Mount Ararat, diffused pink and blue, ethereal, almost surreal, at dawn. There was nobody but ourselves at the little airport – no café, no shop, nothing. We settled down to wait. One hour passed, then two, then three. I demanded that the guide find out what had caused this delay. We'd had no breakfast and by this time were very hungry. Vita, in a long brown garment, got busy with her tiny water heater making cup after cup of Nescafé using a plug in the wall. The guides returned, saying, 'Nobody knows.'

Incensed, I demanded to be taken to the manager of the airport. 'But nobody does that here! You can never ask to see officials. You just have to wait until the plane comes.' Even more incensed, I started out along the corridor, looking for an official.

Tanya was very agitated. 'You cannot do that here, I promise you!' But armoured with my Western 'freedom', I continued. A man in a uniform with many braids attached came out of a door.

'Is that the manager? Ask him why we have been waiting so long. Where is the plane? Give us an explanation.' The official avoided all eye contact. Tanya spoke to him in Russian. 'He does not know.'

'What? Does a manager of an airport not know what's happening to the plane? This is ridiculous. Tell him that we feel extremely insecure.' Perhaps we would be there forever. Without any other sign of having heard, the official disappeared behind a door. 'Right, Tanya, ring up Intourist and tell them to bring a bus here at once to take us to the Matenadaran Library, which we never got time to see.'

'But the plane would come when you have gone. You do not know what they are like here. They would leave you here without a toothbrush. They do not care about you.' This criticism, so imprudent, had been forced out of her.

Nevertheless, I insisted on the bus. The Matenadaran Library was world famous for its collection of ancient Armenian scripts. We rushed up the steps of the library and had barely ten minutes to look around when Tanya appeared, panting and agitated.

'The plane has arrived. You must go at once.' We rushed back to the coach and onwards to the airport. We were rushed up the gangway to the plane without any of the usual demands for our papers or identity. We'd had to wait ten hours for that plane. We never found out where it came from or why it was late.

# The Basalt City

*1979*

After a long, hot journey, we finally reached our destination, the town of Diyarbakir deep in southeast Turkey on the banks of the River Tigris. It is thought to be one of the oldest cities in the world and, as it occupies a strategic position between East and West, has suffered invasion after invasion over the centuries. When we visit, it is still not at peace. It's a hotbed of Kurdish rebellion against the Turkish government, which was particularly dangerous now that the whole country was in a state of near anarchy.

We were tired and looking forward to getting into our hotel. Some half a mile or more from the town, we began to notice an unpleasant smell in the bus. It got stronger and more offensive by the minute. We drew up at a wayside café for information and learned that the refuse collectors of Diyarbakir were on strike. The strike had already lasted six weeks, and in that hot climate, the smell of burning, rotting vegetables and worse was so pungent that we were overcome. The local people were burning all that it was possible to burn, but there was plenty still lying about. At this news, the busboy came down the bus and doused us liberally with his cheap eau-de-cologne. Atila, always in command of every situation, gave the order: we would go straight to our hotel and not come out of it until the next morning, when we would leave directly for Van. But there were those of us foolhardy enough to go against his advice. We had made the long journey to see this strange, black, remote Kurdish town, and see it we would. Some eight of us covered our noses and mouths with handkerchiefs and set out.

Diyarbakir was very impressive, even behind its line of smouldering rubbish. The huge black basalt walls surrounding the town were grimly forbidding. They are said to be second in length to the Great Wall of China. We passed through one of the great gates which gave access to the city and found ourselves in a maze of small streets. Men strolled about in their baggy Kurdish trousers and the few women visible were heavily shrouded in black chadors. In no time at all, we found ourselves surrounded by a swarm of children, avidly curious about this unusual phenomenon – Western tourists. They pulled at us, fingered our watches, lifted our skirts to see what we were wearing underneath, tried to pull open our handbags to see what was inside. We were being picked at from all sides and becoming overpowered, not by the smell, but by the children.

Then, a little girl of about ten years old took command of the situation. She was meagrely dressed but had bright, intelligent eyes. She was carrying in her hand two small eggs which her mother had sent her out to buy. She took hold of my hand and in simple Turkish she asked me where we wanted to go. When she understood that we wanted to see the museum, she shooed off the other children, some of them older than herself, and led us along the narrow streets to the museum. It was closed. She was not deterred. She knocked, banging with her little fist until finally there was a sound of steps and the big door was grudgingly half opened. 'Closed, do you hear? Closed!' The little girl made a sign to my handbag and then to the official at the door. I understood at once. I offered him money. The door was opened and we went inside. The little girl's eyes gleamed with satisfaction at her success. We went through the rooms, looking at the exhibits, the little girl clinging to my hand all the time. After a hasty visit, we went outside again and the little girl steered us along the streets, past the long line of burning rubbish and the appalling smell, and back to our hotel. I brought her into the foyer and was about to bring her up to my room when the receptionist stepped forward. A little native like her was not allowed into the hotel. I was mortified for her. There was no use expostulating: he was adamant. I ran up to my room and brought down some little presents I had stowed away for just such an occasion. She took them with the utmost grace and dignity. We exchanged addresses. She then departed, still clutching her two eggs. When I got back to

Ireland, I sent her a parcel. She replied, her teacher having composed a few English sentences. She enclosed a small, simple tablemat which she had embroidered herself. Many years later, she wrote to tell me that she had graduated in medicine from Istanbul University. The state had paid for her education, in return for which she would have to practise medicine for two years in eastern Turkey.

When we returned to Istanbul, we read that a well-known Turkish journalist who had gone to Diyarbakir to report on the Kurdish rebels had been shot dead in the very hotel where we had stayed and where we had conversed with him.

In our party was an American art historian named Lucinda who was sharing a room with an elderly woman from Belfast. They were a most unlikely pair, but their love of cigarettes had destined them to be together in the same bedroom. Lucinda was tall, chic, travelled, experienced. Miss Kerr was very short, unchic and inexperienced, although well travelled and widely read. I wondered how they would get on together. Lucinda and Miss Kerr always sat side by side in the bus and always in the same seat, just behind the driver, who was a good-looking Turk of about forty. He was very fastidious and very professional towards us. His claim to fame came from his having been a member of the Turkish football team. We all liked him, but I noticed that he and Lucinda took every opportunity to be together. I noticed, too, that Lucinda always kicked off her shoes when she took her seat in the bus. I then noticed from my seat diagonally opposite her that the driver had one hand off the wheel and slyly caressed the feet of Lucinda behind him. My eyes went to Miss Kerr. Did she notice? I saw her eyes fixed, fascinated, at what was going on. She didn't move and said nothing. I said nothing.

One afternoon, I came upon Miss Kerr wandering alone in the town. I hailed her. How was she getting on with Lucinda? 'Oh, very well, exceedingly well. She hasn't come out this afternoon, she told me that she wanted to wash her hair and do the few things that a girl needs to do and have space around her and asked me if I would mind absenting myself for two hours. Of course, I obliged. She's very good to me, insists on giving me cigarettes and wine.' (I knew that Miss Kerr was fond of these two items and that she was reluctant to spend her own money on them.) I guessed that the driver would be 'washing his hair' at the same time.

At the end of the holiday, I asked Miss Kerr if she had enjoyed herself. 'Have you learned much about Turkey?' She looked at me very meaningfully. 'Oh, yes. I've learned a great deal, not only about Turkey, but about other things as well!' I knew that the 'other things' were the real aspects of Miss Kerr's education in eastern Turkey.

As we bowled along in our bus, mile after mile all day long, we watched the landscape unfold, the hills getting higher and higher, the villages smaller and smaller. The climate in eastern Turkey is hard and unforgiving. In winter, the snow lies for months on end, and in summer, the sun blazes down on a scorched land. We could see the flat roofs of the houses and the women laying out peppers and chillies in long rows to dry for use in the winter months. They wore the wide, baggy trousers which women here had worn for centuries, doing the same work; their expectations of life hadn't changed. I thought of Tess of the D'Urbervilles in Hardy's novel. In the beautiful and fertile Wessex, she, too, did the work of women which was centuries old, milking and dairy work. She was seduced by a young man and had a baby. When she married another educated man with whom she was passionately in love, she told him on her wedding night of the seduction and of the baby (who died). He, the liberal, agnostic, so-called free-thinker, abjured her.

Was there a Tess in this rural Turkey? I was sure there was, for human nature is the same everywhere. I had caught a glimpse of some beautiful faces in the village, lovely even behind their headscarves. Surely there were men to desire them. The fate of a Turkish Tess, however, could be much worse than that of an English one. Marriages here were arranged by parents and no physical or sexual contact was allowed beforehand. The price of an illegitimate child could be as high as the killing of the mother by her menfolk.

At midday, we came to a stop for lunch at a small hotel in a wild landscape. Our guide had appointed two o'clock as our time of departure, and at that hour we were back in our seats, ready to resume our journey. Lucinda and the driver were missing. Five past two, ten past two, fifteen minutes past two and the driver and Lucinda came walking back together, the driver looking sheepish and Lucinda not at all. They took their seats without a word of apology. No one said anything. We guessed very well what had been going on.

Suddenly a deep, English public school voice sounded from the back of the bus: 'It is not our business to provide concubines for the driver!' It was our professor of Greek. There was a shocked silence. To use the word 'concubine' was an insult too far. A row broke out. Lucinda, an American, was not going to be thus abused by an upper-class Englishman. Their exchange was hot and barbed. They didn't speak to each other for the remainder of the tour.

In our travels to the Middle East, we were to hear of civilisations we had never heard of before, people who had once been strong, artistic, enterprising, successful traders. They had come and gone over millennia, leaving their buildings, their gods and their artwork behind them for posterity to discover and interpret. Ireland, on the edge of Europe, has seen few invaders, but in the Middle

East, Scythians, Cimmerians, Assyrians, Urartians, Romans, Mongols, Arabs and Turks, among others, had invaded and stayed until more powerful cultures had ousted and replaced them.

Hittites were brought to our attention. I had heard of only one Hittite – Uriah, the Hittite in the Old Testament, who was married to the beautiful Bathsheba. King David, who had fallen in love with Bathsheba, had Uriah sent into the front line of battle, where he was sure to be killed and leave David free to have Bathsheba. He was to repent later in sackcloth and ashes. The Hittites had no more reality for me than the Amalakites, the Perrizites or the other –ites. So it was with the rest of the world until the middle of the nineteenth century.

The story of the discovery of the Hittite Empire, some three thousand years after its disappearance, is very dramatic. While excavating in Syria, a Swiss archaeologist noticed some stones with hieroglyphic writing on them in a wall in the town at Hama. Alerted, he looked about and saw other similar stones – one on a shop wall, another on a house wall and so on. He suspected that he had found something important. He had the stones prised out and sent to be examined by experts in Istanbul. Archaeological detectives set to work.

Having studied them, Professor Saya, Professor of Assyriology at Oxford University, came to the startling conclusion that, some three thousand years earlier, a powerful empire must have existed in the Middle East, possessing its own special artistic culture and its own special script. His investigation led him to Hattusas in central Turkey, where he found a large number of clay tablets similar to those found in Hama, tablets of the Royal Palace in the Royal Archives of Hattusas. These tablets were only deciphered in the 1920s. They were the archives of the Hittite people, a people entirely forgotten to history. These Hittites flourished for over a thousand years in Asia Minor and Syria. They had a well-ordered society and system of laws. They worshipped gods for whom they built great open-air temples. They had over a thousand gods, but they especially worshipped Teshub, the storm god, and Hepatu, the sun goddess.

We visited their capital city, Hattusas, and their open-air religious sanctuary, Yazilkaya. There were no other tourists; we felt like intruders, voyeurs of a civilisation that had managed to keep itself secret and inviolate for thousands of years. We found ourselves reluctant to clamber over this eerie and rugged site, over the walls, foundations of buildings, drainage system, tunnels of a huge city where so long ago a people had been born, lived and died with a model of the world and the universe so different from ours. Their gods stood out in strong relief in ceremonial procession on the huge walls. One thousand years before Christ, they propitiated the elements here, the storm and sun gods. It was their holiest religious sanctuary and the burial place of their kings. We had no right to be there.

We learned that these same Hittites had fought the Egyptians at the Battle of Kadesh in the reign of Rameses II of Egypt, during whose reign the biblical exodus took place. The Egyptians were stopped from further expansion by the Hittites and the Treaty of Kadesh is the first known written peace treaty in history.

What is Turkey without a Turkish rug? Buying a rug in Turkey is an experience not to be missed. Turks have been traders for centuries: it's in their blood, even the children's. Every child is a potential entrepreneur eager and waiting to make a sale, even if only a glass of water. Turks sell by charm – it's the secret of their success, and it works. More than one of us succumb to their incantations.

This is how it happens. You pass a carpet shop and glance inside. In a flash, a Turk is at the door, scenting a customer. 'Where are you from?'

'We are from Ireland.'

'From North or South?'

'From Northern Ireland.'

'Well, I have a friend, Mr Jackson from Cookstown – here is his card.' (It has the name of an insurance company on it.) 'Come in, come in and look around. No need to buy. Just look and admire beautiful things!' He beckons us to seats specially placed along the wall.

'But we have only five minutes. Our guide is waiting for us!'

'Five minutes is enough to look at beautiful

things! You have no money, you say? No need to pay now. Pay when you get home. Pay next year! This is my son Mustapha and my daughter Sayeste. Mustapha will show you a unique piece. Bring tea for our guests!' With a wave of the hand, little trays bearing glasses of apple tea appear. We are now more or less drawn into the family circle. 'This one? Too bright, you say? Oh, I see, lady, you are a connoisseur. You appreciate the antique!' His son unrolls rug after rug. 'I give you a good price. Everybody knows me here as an honest man. Ask Mr Jackson of Cookstown. He will tell you. I am your son, lady!' He kisses his hand and places it on his brow. 'Lady, how much water is pouring from your heart for this rug? Tell me! Tell me! What is your price, lady?' I offer a price. 'Lady, you cannot be serious! This piece, it has taken six months to weave. Look at the number of stitches to the inch! A young Kurdish woman has put her heart into it – for you, lady!' I cannot hold out. Finally, we settle on a price and in a few minutes my rug is reduced by expert hands to a small, manageable parcel. Money is paid. He beats his breast. 'Lady, you come back tomorrow and I show you more beautiful things. Lady, you are my mummy!'

Seasoned by this first encounter, I go the following year to look at another rug shop which has been recommended to us. It is on the other side of the Grand Bazaar and up one flight of steps – a good sign, we thought – the owner wasn't rich enough to have the ground floor, the prime position for sales. We climbed steep stairs and found ourselves in a large room where an elderly Turk was telling his worry beads. He had a very large nose, such as you see in caricatures of Turks, although we saw very few of them in reality. 'You want to see beautiful carpets? I have many unique pieces here. No need to buy. Just look, please. You are English ladies on holiday in Turkey?'

'No, we're Irish.'

'You are Irish, you say. Which part, North or South?' We were impressed by his knowledge of Ireland and our political situation. 'North? Ah, you are Protestants, then! Ladies, you can trust me. I am a Protestant, too. In fact, I am a Presbyterian.'

We baulked at this gross piece of marketing. 'How can you be a Presbyterian?' I asked, waiting for some artistic reply.

'I was educated by Presbyterian missionaries in Turkey, so I am a Presbyterian!' It was not impossible, given his age. Did Presbyterians go as missionaries to Turkey? 'And lady, as I said, you can trust me. In a court of law in Turkey, a Muslim must swear on the Koran, an orthodox on the Bible, but a Presbyterian is never asked to swear at all. His word is enough.' We were astonished.

With a wave of his hand, apple tea appeared. As we sipped, we realised we were being made to feel some sort of Presbyterian complicity with this man, yet neither of us was Presbyterian! 'I show you unique piece. The people keep them for me because they trust me to give them a good price.' As he spoke, his assistant unrolled rug after rug, while he looked into our faces for the slightest sign of interest which he could instantly cultivate. We fell before temptation. We didn't know enough to judge. We felt obliged to buy something from this 'Presbyterian'. The deal was done and we left well satisfied with our bargains. When we unrolled our treasures at home, we found them carelessly woven and frayed at the edges. We had been 'done'. My friend was furious, as she prided herself on her discernment. Her *amour-propre* was deeply offended. Mine was only dented. I sewed up the frayed edges and put my Presbyterian rug down in my hall, where it lasted many years.

# Moscow
## 1981

Having seen Leningrad, we wanted to see Moscow, which is claimed to be the real heart of Russia and is a city which features in many of Tolstoy's novels. On the first morning we have been 'summoned', our guide tells us, to a round table conference this morning. It's a very important event. The head of the English-speaking Moscow radio is to meet us, as well as a well-known economist from the university and several other important people. 'They want to make you welcome here in the Soviet Union and to explain their system to you.' We were amazed – a party of tourists from Northern Ireland to be thus summoned!

It was with great curiosity that we entered the room and took our seats at the round table, which was obviously used for such events. A small version of our national flag had been placed in the middle of the table – though it was green, white and yellow! They hadn't done their homework. We looked at one another and smiled and said nothing.

Yes, we could ask any questions we liked. Theirs was a 'free' society. We knew better than to say anything that smacked of criticism of the system, but one of our young boys put up his hand to ask a question. We were horrified!

'How do you explain the resistance of the people to Soviet soldiers in Afghanistan in 1979? They must have had a cause.'

We drew our breath. The answer was unagitated, even bland: 'Would not any country – *your* country – resist brutal terrorists?'

The moment passed.

# The Golden Road to Samarkand

## *1982*

To see 'the golden road to Samarkand' was a poetic invitation. To see the city of Tamburlaine the Terrible, its magnificent mosques and palaces, to see its peoples who live in a remote desert and to experience what communism had done to the Uzbek people.

> *We travel not for trafficking alone*
> *By hotter winds our fiery hearts are fanned.*
> *For lust of knowing what should not be known*
> *We take the Golden Road to Samarkand.*

Thus Samarkand, in these lines from James Elroy Flecker, entered the imagination of our adolescent lives. We hardly knew what the lines meant. Samarkand was an exotic name to roll around on the tongue, a mystical, magical, dream-like place unanchored in time and space. In 1982, it was almost a shock to learn that Samarkand was a real place and could be visited. Intourist Moscow offered a visit to Central Asia which included Bokkara and Samarkand. We had to consult the map to see where they were.

Central Asia was an enormous, unknown secret country whose size baffled the imagination. It was somewhere to the north of Iran, west of China and east of the Caspian Sea. Great plains sloped down over thousands of miles to that sea. Big rivers fed by glaciers from huge mountains never succeeded in reaching the ocean, but vanished into landlocked seas, residual waters collected into lakes such as Lake Balkash and the Aral Sea. To the ordinary European consciousness, these great tracts of land were savage, wild and uncultivated, yet its cities were older than Russian cities and its art and architecture went back to the Bronze Age. Moreover, it hadn't been isolated – the Silk Road traversed it on its way from the Far East to Europe and brought many cultural influences with it over the centuries. Its cities were attacked, ravaged and often changed hands. Alexander the Great reached Central Asia in the third century BC, the Arabs conquered it in the seventh century AD, the Mongols in the thirteenth century and the Russians in 1868. The Bolsheviks took it over in 1921 and made five geographically artificial republics out of it – Uzbekistan, Kazakstan, Turkmenistan, Kyrgystan and Tajistan. The Soviets shut down thousands of mosques and these republics were turned from being Muslim to being communist states. Or were they? It would be interesting to find out.

We travelled by plane from the Crimea to Tashkent, and in that four-hour journey we saw Central Asia unroll itself beneath us, desert everywhere, interrupted by the Sea of Azov and the Caspian Sea, with Batu protruding into it as it did on our maps – always a surprise for me. As we emerged from the plane in Tashkent, we felt an unaccustomed heat. There was no sign of the Hindu Kush or Pamir Mountains, although the guidebook promised that we would land at the foot of them.

We were off the next morning to Bokkara and Samarkand. We could visit Tashkent, a modern city, on our way back. The flight took us over immense, flat desert with green oases clearly defined here and there against the bleached sand and mud brick villages which, unchanged in colour or design over the centuries, barely defined themselves against the desert.

Bokkara was unlike any other city we had ever seen. But for the TV masts rising up among the prayer flags outside the walls, we might have been looking at a fossil from the Middle Ages. Entering the Old Town, we saw the big pool, built in 1620, which constituted the city's only water supply and brought disease with it. Running water only came to the town in the 1930s. Mosque after mosque, medressah (theological school) after medressah, told us that this was the most religious city on the Silk Route. Its one hundred religious colleges and nearly four hundred mosques were all shut down by the communists. The old centre is still lived in, in narrow dark streets where small houses are pressed together and large, faded wooden doors

open to courtyards where, here and there, a plant
blooms and a bed is laid out in the shade. The
lovely metal domes of the Bazaar remind us that
this town was a great trading centre as well as a
deeply religious one. Now only storks nest in the
high vantage points of the domes and minarets.
We heard no familiar call to prayer, so sign of religious life anywhere except for an old man praying
in the gallery of what was obviously a 'permitted'
medressah. Religion has gone underground, yet
the city has a peculiar atmosphere of quietness, almost of secrecy. No one pays any attention to us
few tourists. People go about their business as if
we aren't there. They hold themselves erect and
proud. The men wear the *chasma* on their heads,
the women silk caftans and trousers in the traditional broken rainbow design. They wear their hair
in long dark braids, because shorn hair is not ac-
ceptable to Uzbeks.

Bokkara is an extraordinary city, a city which,
until 1920, lived as it had since medieval times.
When the Russians arrived in 1920, they brought
buses with them. The people didn't know what to
do with them and sat down on the floor between
the seats. The vast, gloomy bulk of the Ark, the
Palace Fortress of the Emirs (the last fled in 1920),
now rose up before us. The Emirs ruled here by
sheer terror and executed on a whim; absolute
power was used until 1920. As we climbed the
ramp up to the entrance of that forbidden palace
and walked down the tunnel inside, we could feel

the fear seeping from the torture chambers: 'A hundred deaths a day,' said the guide. Remains of courtyards, sumptuous halls and harems spoke of the extreme conjunction of beauty and cruelty in these Central Asian cities.

Colonel Stoddart, an Englishman, visited Bokkara on a diplomatic mission. He was thrown into a lice-infested pit for having unknowingly insulted the Emir, where he languished in frightful conditions for three years. In 1841, Captain Connolly, an Irishman of the Bengal Light Cavalry, came to rescue him. He, too, was thrown into the pit. They both refused to become Muslims. In 1842, they were marched into the square and made to dig their own graves. They embraced, declared themselves Christians and were beheaded with a knife. Friends and relatives of the unfortunate men sent out a clergyman named Joseph Wolff to find out the truth. Wolff might have shared the same fate had not the Emir thought him hilariously funny in his full clerical regalia and let him go.

The cotton harvest – 'white gold' – was going forward everywhere in the communes, but on the edge of the town there was a barricade of police stopping cars and pedestrians, checking their papers to see if they were trying to avoid the harvest. They had to be locked in to do it!

I asked where I might buy a Bokkara rug. Bokkara rugs? Did I not know that under the communists, all home industry was a crime?

That evening, the floor lady in the hotel, a small, handsome Uzbek woman, offered to make me tea. She began by throwing hot water out of the teapot all over the floor, where it steamed and hissed. When the tea was infused, she poured more hot water over the teapot, which again ran liberally over the floor. She has eight children, she tells me, and she hates the Russians.

That evening, we were present in an open court-yard of a mosque to see Uzbek folk dancing. We sat in the indigo light of the desert on raised plat-forms which hold about eight people and which the guide called 'the national beds', watching in the floodlight the highly subtle, restrained classical dances of this ancient people. The Soviets have always encouraged local folk customs, but never national feeling.

Our journey from Bokkara to Samarkand was to be by train. Our compartments, 'soft class', were luxurious with heavy wooden panelling, stainless steel fitments, white sheets and tea in glasses. We reached Samarkand at 2 a.m. to find that there were no bedrooms available for six of us. Six volunteers, including myself and the Professor of Modern History, lay down side by side in the lobby. At 5.30 a.m. we were awoken to the news that our beds were ready. Two hours' sleep, then breakfast, and we were off to visit the dream city of Samarkand.

Its buildings are much more sensational in size and design than those of Bokkara. Tamburlaine himself designed Samarkand as a showpiece. He was born some sixty miles south of the city. After devastating Persia, Russia, India, Syria and Asia Minor, he returned to his beloved Samarkand. He was determined to build a city there that would be the glory of the world. To this end, he brought architects, scholars, silk weavers, tile-makers and calligraphers to build magnificent mosques, medressahs, bazaars and libraries, while he, ever the nomad, lived in a tent on the plains. Although he could neither read nor write, he had a thirst for learning and discussed history, medicine, mathematics and astronomy with learned men. Although Samarkand has suffered invasions, earthquakes and war over the centuries as well as the ravages of neglect, it is still a brilliant, even theatrical city. Everything is calculated to attract the eye. The huge mosques and medressahs are arranged in perfect symmetry with their vestments of gold, tile and script, sumptuous yet subordinated to the whole like a perfect poem, the geometrical patterns of the natural universe caught for a while in bricks, mosaic and majolica. It's difficult here in Registan Square to imagine the gallop of Tamburlaine's nomad horsemen.

Only one mosque, the Shir Dor, with its startling (for Muslim non-personal art) representation of the Sun God with Mongol features and tigers in frontal positions, brings Tamburlaine the tiger to sudden life. Nearby, the Bibi-Khanym mosque, the great mosque of Samarkand, now in near ruins, tells the story, legend says, of how Muslim women came to wear the veil. While Tamburlaine was away on campaign, his Chinese wife, Bibi Khanym, planned to build a mosque as a surprise for her husband. The architect of the mosque fell madly in love with her and demanded a kiss, which she accorded. When Tamburlaine returned, he saw the mark of the kiss on her face, executed the architect and decreed that all Muslim women should henceforth use the veil.

It seemed impossible to believe that such a man as Tamburlaine could have died a mortal's death, yet he is buried here in Samarkand, in the beautiful Gur Emir mosque. A large, understated slab of dark black-green jade marks his tomb, looking strangely restrained under the highly decorated dome above. His tomb was opened and shut again by a Soviet anthropologist in 1942, who claimed that the body in the tomb was lame in his left foot – Tamburlaine means Timur the Lame, a true appellation, it seems.

Strangely, it was the necropolis of Shah-I-Zinda which most deeply impressed me in Samarkand. Tamburlaine had it built to house the bodies of his friends and relations. We walked up the long street of the dead – mausoleums to the right of us, mausoleums to the left of us, all now crumbling away, the domes, bare now, having lost their vestments by earthquake and neglect over time, yet to me even more beautiful by being bare. The whole thing has been dug out by archaeologists from the mountain of earth which engulfed it. We can see a small cliff at the back which marked the height of the enveloping earth before excavation. The domes and walls may be half-crumbled away, but script – the Word of God and source of all knowledge – combines in classical perfection with rosettes and arabesques, moving from one scale to another and as finely mapped as the patterns of the universe itself. This a holy place for Muslims – we see a few older pilgrims holding hands. They have come to visit the place where the Prophet's cousin, Kussam-ibn-Abbas, on delivering his last sermon, jumped into a well where he still lives – Shah-I-Zinda, the living king, is the name of the necropolis.

That evening, we sat on benches in the square in front of Tamburlaine's great mosque, and as the indigo blue darkness of the desert descended on us, Son et Lumière acted out the life and final destiny of Tamburlaine himself with a thunder of hooves, screams and death howls. Somehow, it was artificial, unconvincing, unmoving. It might have been taking place in any one of the castles of the Loire Valley. Tamburlaine was absent.

Tamburlaine's grandson, Ulugh Beg, sounds like an Ulster chieftain. In fact, he was a mathematician and astronomer. He had a three-storey observatory constructed, built along a huge sextant and set along the meridian. There, he calculated the rotation of the globe and was only one minute out. Although a scholar, he was involved in a power struggle with the Chief Priest, who claimed that he taught classes of girls. Ulugh Beg was sent to Mecca and beheaded on his way back. He left behind a catalogue of the stars, 1,180 of them. It was fascinating to see the long, semi-circular channel in the ground where this Mongol looked up and out at the universe with avid, scientific eyes, whereas his grandfather, Tamburlaine, had looked upon the terrestrial conquest of the world here below as his ultimate ambition.

The remote town of Khiva was our next objective. In 1980, very few people made the journey to see this living fossil of a city. Although isolated in the middle of broad deserts, it was once a thriving trading post on the Silk Road. The Khans became so puffed up with wealth that they came to think of themselves as invincible. Their wealth, however, came from a huge market in slaves. In 1717, Russia sent a delegation of four hundred men to Khiva. The Khivites massacred every one of them. The Russians had their revenge in 1873, when a 13,000-strong force took the town. In 1920, it was absorbed into the Uzbek Socialist Republic and withered away.

A plane flight to Urgench brought us to this remote fossil of a town. Its huge, curved defensive mud walls, prayer flags and TV masts spanned the centuries in the most incongruous mix. Old women squatted beside stalls of cheap local ware traditionally designed, hoping for a sale to us few tourists. Inside the walls, the many mosques and medressahs told us that this city was also an important theological centre. They stand in dramatic contrast to the savage walls, the torture chambers of the Ark, seat of the Khans, and the large market for slaves near the East Gate. What terrible horrors went on here, as accounts of men have left us – the gouging out of eyes, the collection of heads from beheaded victims, mouths being slit open and women tied up in sacks with wild cats. It's estimated that there were as many as 30,000 slaves on offer at any one time. This regime only came to an end in 1920, in the lifetime of people still living.

After dinner in the hotel in Urgench, a live orchestra played dance music. There was only one other tourist group present, a French party. All of our group got up to dance, but the French remained seated. I went to their table and invited them to join us. On hearing that we were Irish, not English, they relaxed, talked, got up and danced. Yes, they were here for the same reason as ourselves, to see Khiva. They had found it as fascinating as we had. They were departing the next morning after breakfast, but we were to spend the morning in the Kizilkhum desert. At breakfast the next morning, the French had already left. We had the hotel to ourselves.

The desert was a great surprise. It was neither the huge sandy dunes of the Sahara nor the dead-looking parts of the Gobi. It was alive with growing things. It was once a sea bed and was still saturated with salt. For anything to grow in it, the salt had to be washed out twice a year, a huge task. Marron grasses have been introduced to hold the soil together and some shrubs have adapted themselves to the salty conditions. Occasional salt flats shone like hoar frost. The air was fresh and lightsome, like a spring day in Ireland. Birds sang cheerfully and wild flowers showed in blue, yellow and white clumps. Pools of water lay all about us, their shining levels taking and giving back their colours to the clear sky above. As we lifted the clear water to our lips, the salt of that sunken sea bed was sharp and tangy on our tongues. We sat on the bank of a salt lake and listened to the humming of the bees. The pale turquoise blue of the sky lay cool and motionless on the waters of the deep jade irrigation channels which were deepened at the side by the shadows cast by the large dunes which resembled a castle more than a Khivan defence wall. At intervals, a fish broke the surface of the waters. Delicate fronds of plants on which camels feed showed pale green and grey in the colours of Donegal. We sat silent, entranced. The final tribute came from Angeline: 'It's just like Fermanagh on a fine day!'

At lunch, we were the only tourists in the dining room. Two or three lone men ate at small tables nearby. As we talked together of all we had seen and heard, a waitress started to lay out bottles of champagne on our tables. 'But we didn't order champagne!' we cried.

Our guide, Tanya, was obliged to explain. 'Someone has fallen in love with your party and wants to offer you champagne.'

'But who is it? Tell us please, or we cannot drink it.'

'I have been sworn to secrecy,' said Tanya, smiling. At once, I thought of the departed French. 'No,' said Tanya, 'it was not the French.' On our continued insistence, Tanya had to speak. 'Do you see that young man sitting alone at a table by the window? He is a sailor in the Soviet Navy.' We noticed his weather-beaten face and could believe it. 'About six months ago, his ship was wrecked in the White Sea. He would have certainly lost his life in those icy waters but for the speedy aid of a British ship which picked him up and set him ashore at Murmansk. He has never been able to thank them properly. You are the first English people he has met since that day and he wants to thank them through you!'

We were amazed and insisted that he join us at our table, which he did shyly and reluctantly. Tanya translated the story of his shipwreck and he soon relaxed. We toasted Russia, England, the Soviet Navy, the Royal Navy and anything else we could think of. There, in that remote corner of the Khilkum desert, we experienced, not for the first time, the generous spirit of the Russian people.

# A Sore Thumb in Luxor

## 1984

Egypt, where everything began! It was hot. All morning we had walked around the huge temples of Luxor and Karnak, listened attentively to our guide and marvelled at what the pharaohs had achieved. After lunch, Jane and I went together to explore the market, that never-failing, fascinating complex of colours, textures and smells. As we passed a small carpet shop, a handsome young Egyptian, who was obviously the owner, was sitting outside it, nursing a sore thumb. I had absolutely determined not to go into carpet shops, knowing my great weakness in that direction. More than once, I had fallen before temptation in Turkey.

I couldn't help but look sympathetically at this man's pain, for his face was contorted and he couldn't seem to manage to put the bandage securely on his thumb. I leaned over and helped him secure it. He smiled his thanks and insisted on us going into his shop so that he could express his thanks in the form of a present. We passed through one small room packed with folded rugs, then through another where a burly Egyptian passively stood – a security man, I thought. He led us past the man and into a third room, also packed with folded rugs on shelves. He began to look around for our 'present' when suddenly he turned, threw his arms around me, pulled me to him and covered my faces with kisses. 'I give you good sex, ma'am, good sex!' I struggled, shouted. He held me in a vice and ran his hands all over me. I noticed that his bandage had fallen off his thumb and that there was nothing wrong with it!

We struggled so violently that we fell sideways against the rugs and they all fell down on top of us. My companion, sensing an opportune moment, ran out past the 'security' man and through the front room, leaving me to fend for myself. I began to get really frightened. I was too far from the street outside for my screams to be heard and I was alone with an amorous Egyptian. We struggled and fought and more and more rugs fell on us until we were in a sea of rugs. In an attempt to keep the remaining rugs in place, he leaned back against them. I gave him a kick with all my might, aiming specifically at his vulnerable parts as far as I could guess under his loose habit and ran out past the security man, through the front shop and into freedom. I was shaken but unharmed and could even see the funny side of my adventure. I had been taken in by a sore thumb!

# Georgia, Land of Myth and Snow

*1984*

Prometheus, by legend chained to a rock in the Caucasus Mountains, Jason and the Golden Fleece and Stalin, born there and educated in a seminary – all of this was to send us to Georgia.

Looking down from the plane over the famous Caucasus Mountains, I could see a long chain of chiselled, snow-covered mountain peaks and hidden valleys. This chain strides all the way from the Black Sea to the Caspian Sea and forms Russia's most southerly border. In these valleys, forty languages are spoken by different tribes. The northern Caucasus was taken over by Russia early in the nineteenth century and at the time of the Bolshevik Revolution was completely absorbed. Georgia, in the southern part of the Caucasus, has had an independent kingdom since the days of Herodotus and was Christianised very early on, in the fourth century, in spite of numerous invasions by other cultures. Georgians are known for their ferocious independence of spirit. Now it was a Soviet Republic, but very different from other Soviet Republics, as we were about to see.

For us Western Europeans, the Caucasus is, above all, the land of myth and legend. It was here that Prometheus dared to bring down fire from heaven to humankind. He was punished by the gods by being chained to a rock on Mount Elbruz (which we could see from the plane) where, every day, his liver was picked over by vultures only to grow again at night to be picked to pieces again the next day, a myth that lends itself to powerful analogies. It was here, too, that Jason sailed with the Argonauts in pursuit of the Golden Fleece. The king of Colchis's daughter, Medea, fell in love with Jason and agreed to help him. But the gods put a spell on her and she betrayed her country and deceived her father. The pair married and had children. Finally, Jason betrayed her for another, more politically advantageous woman. She took a terrible revenge: she killed not only the other woman, but her three children by Jason. The Caucasus was a place of terror, punishment and revenge.

The word 'Georgia' does not come from St George, as I had thought, as this saint is greatly venerated there, but from the world *'gurf'* or *'jurf'*. Neither do the people call themselves Georgians, but Kartivelians, and their land Sa-Kartel after a pagan god called Kartos who is said to be the father of all Georgians. Their language is not Russian and they are not Slavs.

Our guide, Tanya, looked after us in Moscow. When we got to the airport for our flight to Tbilisi, we found we had two more guides, giving us three in all. We were going far away from the centre, so one guide would have been sent to watch the others: they might be buying dollars, sending messages, fraternising with tourists or other dangerous pursuits. On the plane, I found myself sitting beside Tanya No. 2. She was smartly dressed, cold, self-possessed and bored. To make conversation, I asked her, 'Is this your full-time job? Where did you learn your excellent English?'

She looked coldly at me. 'Not full time. I work for my father.'

'What does he do, your father?'

She looked through me. 'Let us say that he is in electronic communications.' I read the code – he was in bugging devices. She might just as well have said 'Keep off! You do not interest me. I am bored stiff with your group already.'

Coming out of Tbilisi Airport was like entering another world from Moscow. People were going about their business confidently, cheerfully, like free people with none of the taciturnity of the Russians. On the way to our hotel, I noticed the many cars on the road and a huge second-hand car market. 'So many cars?' I asked.

'Yes, everyone here has a car, wants a car, wants a better car. We make money. We buy cars. We grow early vegetables in this mild climate and send plane-loads of them up to Moscow every day!' In return, the Russians leave them alone.

Georgians are not only fiercely independent, they are also artistic and their language is extremely rich. Pasternak said of them what might also be said of the Irish: 'vivid colloquial language, ancient legends all make poets of the people'. This did not stop Stalin from sending many of them to the gulags, though.

We made our way to the restaurant in our hotel, Ivernia. A group of Georgian men were eating, drinking, talking and laughing at the next table. While we were considering their lean, handsome, tall figures, their black hair and blue eyes, so unlike the heavy Slav features, a waitress approached and started to lay out bottles of champagne on our tables. 'This champagne is a present from the men at the next table. They welcome you as tourists to their country. They are the Tbilisi football team and they are celebrating a recent victory.' We turned, we exclaimed, we smiled, we clapped our hands in appreciation. In seconds, they were all seated at our tables.

'Where are you from? Ireland?' Yes, they knew about Belfast. Bang, bang, Belfast! Yes, they knew George Best, Georgie the Best. One of the men took his napkin from the table and flung it on the floor. 'That,' he said, 'is Georgia.' He then put his foot on the napkin and ground it into the floor. 'And that,' he said, 'is Russia.' He flung another napkin onto the floor. 'That,' he said, 'is Ireland.' He repeated the stamping into the floor. 'And that,' he said, 'is England.' There was no use saying anything – better to toast our common victimhood in good Georgian champagne.

I have never breathed such invigorating air as in the Caucasus Mountains. We had already had lungfuls of it on the Military Highway, which runs through these mountains. That morning, we were to go high into the mountains again to visit a famous city, Kutaisi. We were all seated in the bus. The guide protested. 'It is hard to go to. It might be all closed!' We insisted. Finally, the truth came out – we were not going to Kutaisi because we had been ordered to go instead to Stalin's birthplace, Gori. This surprised us, because we knew that Stalin had had thousands of his fellow Georgians killed or sent to the gulags in the great purges of the 1930s. They surely could not love him. The guide was adamant. We must go to Gori. We were astonished to see pictures of Stalin affixed to the windows of the bus. We reached Gori speculating about this phenomenon.

Gori is a small town with a huge Doric temple in the middle. The son of a drunken cobbler, Stalin left the small two-roomed house at fifteen to be educated as a priest in the local seminary. He was banished when they found him reading Victor Hugo. Little did they know he was reading Marx as well! During the 1930s, Gori was redesigned. Several hundred houses were demolished to make room so that one could take pre-eminence: Stalin's birthplace and house museum. The tiny house Stalin lived in until he was fifteen is in front of the museum proper, perfectly preserved and with its own temple built around it. There, in the half-dark, with no notices in English, we followed Stalin's career as far as the Yalta Conference. We gazed with wonder at Stalin's eerie death-mask laid out in a separate room. To one side of the museum is the train carriage Stalin used to travel to the Potsdam Conference in 1945. It is simple, dignified and bullet-proof.

When Stalin's body was removed from the Red Square Mausoleum in 1961, people in Gori mounted a round-the-clock guard on *their* Stalin. 'Why should Stalin be so popular here when he murdered so many of his own people?' I asked.

'Because he is seen as having saved us from the Nazis. He won the Great Patriotic War. Without him, that war would not have been won.' I had heard that many times in the Soviet Union. No doubt there was a lot of truth in it.

# Moscow

*1984*

In 1984, I found myself again in Moscow. Nothing had changed. The city was as bleak, empty and dismal as ever. The only cars to be seen were the same black 'official' cars which crossed Red Square to and from the Kremlin. The square was still immense and lifeless. The shops were still empty and communist inertia reigned supreme. Only the long queue of people waiting to see Lenin's embalmed body in his mausoleum seemed to have a purpose. Yet I knew that in the huge, brutal-style suburbs of the city, women were anything but inert – they were working in factories, bringing up children, searching for food and trying to avoid trouble. Tourists like us didn't get to know them, as foreigners were still taboo. We looked instead at the enchanting cathedrals, the magnificent crops of golden cupolas, elegant crosses and pastel colours which everywhere defied time and communism alike.

I was looking forward to seeing Natasha again. She had been a Russian language assistant for two years in Queen's University, Belfast, where I had got to know her. Intelligent, humorous and witty, she became a firm friend. She would have earned very little money, but what she did earn, she saved rigorously. She wanted to bring goods back to Moscow. She had a special ambition to buy a sewing machine. She spent hardly any money on herself and would have made a small boiling chicken last a week. Everyone liked her. Her background remained vague, however. She had a husband and daughter in Moscow, but we never learned anything about them. She had spent time in other countries, a sure sign of political favour, though she remained pleasantly noncommittal on political issues. She was a mystery. When she learned that I was to be in Moscow, she invited me to a meal in her apartment – it wasn't allowed for her to come visit me in my tourist hotel. She arranged everything. Yuri, a friend and colleague from the university where she taught English, had a car. He would pick me up and take me to her home. He was middle aged and intelligent, with a constant ironic smile on his lips.

'What do you teach in the university?' I asked politely.

'Philosophy,' Yuri replied.

'What branch of philosophy do you specialise in?' I asked.

His ironic smile grew more pronounced. 'Marxist-Leninism, of course!' he replied. I should have known better than to have asked such an inane question.

We drove at speed in his car along dark, straight, deserted roads, rattling in an alarming way in his old banger. Natasha's apartment was one of hundreds in huge, post-war apartment blocks. It was very small – a sparsely furnished living room, a kitchen, bathroom and one bedroom. Natasha considered herself very lucky to have it, as it was difficult to find anywhere to live in Moscow.

Natasha welcomed me warmly. Her daughter Marina, son-in-law Kolya and granddaughter Olga were all there to meet me. In spite of the scarcity of food in Russia, the table was laden. There were delicious wild mushroom pies which she had made herself from mushrooms she had gathered in the fields around her *dacha*, some twenty miles from Moscow. Vodka flowed freely, and although I don't like it, I was obliged to swallow toast after toast. 'A man drinks a bottle of vodka with his meal, a woman half a bottle. We need something to get us through,' I was told. Glasses were raised, smiles exchanged, toasts made in the most effusive terms. Everyone loved everyone else. It was Russian conviviality as I had read of it in novels.

Natasha withdrew for a moment, then returned with a small box in her hands. She had something to show me, she said. The mask of disingenuous political innocence which she had worn for two years in Belfast was about to slip. Her husband had died a short time ago, I knew. Did I know that he had been a lawyer? A lawyer in the army? He had been, of course, a member of the Party, but I must not think that he had been responsible for sending innocent people to gulags or to their deaths. On

the contrary, he had fought hard to have the innocent declared innocent. Moreover, he had fought
all through the war and had gained medals for valour. She displayed his medals with quiet pride. Yuri
had been his friend and knew that she was speaking the truth. Yes, he had fought, not for 'the system', but for Mother Russia. Did I realise that
ordinary Russians had fought like demons in the
war? Ordinary Russians were devoted to their
country as no other people were: 'We have had to
go through terrible hardships, no one will ever
know how many.' Natasha had seen and suffered
so much herself, such as the bombardment of
Moscow by the Germans, who had got to within
twenty-five miles of the city. Only a miracle saved
them. Then there was the starvation, the deadly
cold, disease and death.

She showed me a photograph of her husband,
a distinguished-looking man in military uniform.
In 1983, he developed cancer. She nursed him herself in this tiny apartment. He was in terrible pain
and there were few drugs available to relieve his
suffering. The experience had nearly killed her.
When he died, she had to go into a rest home for
several months to recover. Now she was back to
herself again, 'a strong Russian woman'. She was
proud of her husband.

# Outer Mongolia
## 1984

This vast country seemed more remote than any other country in the world. We wanted to see its limitless grasslands, its wildlife, its shepherds with their flocks, unchanged over the centuries and the hope of the famous Mongol armies, and Genghis Khan.

If there is one name which speaks of primitive energy and violence more than any other, it is Mongolia. In the thirteenth century, the Mongols erupted out of the Asian steppe and by sheer military genius subdued Central Asia, China, Korea, Vietnam, Russia as far as Moscow, Georgia, Armenia, Asia Minor (Turkey), Syria and Jordan, thus creating the biggest empire the world had ever seen. Their capital city was at Karakoram in today's Outer Mongolia, a country practically absent from the consciousness of modern Western people. Yet everybody knows the names of Genghis Khan and Tamburlaine, both of whom have attained almost mythical proportions in the annals of murder and destruction. These names are synonymous with terror, conquest and destruction.

We were now on our way to this wild land of ferocious, visionary conquest by Trans-Siberian train. We rounded the southern end of Lake Baikal and crossed over the border between Soviet Russia and Outer Mongolia. As it was a night journey, we could see little of the Gobi Desert we were traversing, but what looked like a veritable sea of pebbles stretching to infinity. We awoke the next morning to see the great grass ocean all around us that is the steppe, with the snow-capped range of the Atlas Mountains in the far distance. It was clear we were far from all urban civilisation from the number of big birds of prey which inhabited the infinite empty space beneath the sky. Eagles and buzzards dipped, hovered, swooped and rose steeply again and mademoiselle cranes flew in elegant formation. Wild horses ran furiously alongside the train and every now and then groups of nomadic herdsmen followed their flocks, as they had done since time immemorial. These nomadic tribes have no permanent home – they live on the move, sleeping in collapsible tents called yurts as they seek pasture for their flocks. They are unlettered and untutored (Tamburlaine could neither read nor write), yet were capable of conquering and controlling half the known world.

In the thirteenth century, the military genius Genghis Khan galvanised the many Mongol tribes into one and forged them into a highly disciplined and loyal army. Their strength was their cavalry. Mongols were, and still are, brought up on horseback, where they ate, slept, fought and took part in skilful and ferocious games. So precious was a horse that stealing one could lead to execution. Every male

Mongol had to be ready to go to war at any moment. They were expert archers and could shoot backwards or forwards from a galloping horse. They had the best stirrups in the world. Genghis knew the importance of advance information and had a network of spies who sent information along a highly efficient communication system. The horse-riders who carried this information bandaged their bodies against the aching fatigue of hours of hard riding and changed horses as weariness caused horse after horse to falter under them, their own endurance superhuman. They brought terror and destruction to entire populations everywhere they went. They were known as 'the scourge of God'. Here, in these beautiful, empty grasslands, it was hard to imagine the galloping cavalry intent on destruction.

The Mongol empire began to crumble after Genghis's death: 'he that triumphs on horseback cannot rule on horseback'. In the seventeenth century, the Mongols came under a Chinese dynasty. In 1911, China's last dynasty, the Qing, collapsed and Mongolia declared its independence from China. In 1928, the Russians occupied Mongolia and declared it a People's Republic. Under Stalin, the land was collectivised and terrible purges followed. Buddhist monks were murdered and their property seized. By 1939, an estimated 27,000 people had been eliminated. In 1990, encouraged by Gorbachev's perestroika, Mongolia made the transition from a Soviet satellite state to a democracy.

# Brief Encounters

It was in 1984, during the communist period, that we arrived in that extraordinary, forgotten land. A forest of satellite listening stations on the outskirts of Ulan Bator told us that Big Brother was watching. The centre of the town was recognisably communist, consisting of a large square with big, grey, monochrome buildings, a Palace of Culture, a Great Hall of the People, etc. High apartment blocks looked wrong in this landscape.

Old Mongolia was still alive and well, however, in the men, women and children strolling in the streets. Some wore the *del*, or tunic, seen in pictures of the Golden Horde, a robe fixed with buttons at the right shoulder and a silken sash around the waist. Some even wore the leather boots with curled toes which Genghis Khan himself might have worn. Many men and children on horseback crossed the town and the wide gap between the knees of those who were walking told us that they were more accustomed to being on horseback than on foot.

On the outskirts of the city, traditional yurts, or collapsible tents, with brightly coloured front doors housed more people than the apartment blocks. Wrestlers with bulging muscles were practising here and there for the coming yearly festival of Yadarn. Little had changed, it seemed, since the thirteenth century – horse riding, archery and wrestling were still the three prized activities of the Mongols.

We were to stay in Ulan Bator for three days before going on to Datong in China. Our woman guide was big, tough, brisk and very uncharming. There were various things to be seen and she would show them to us, but no more. There was none of the usual response to our interest and curiosity. There was to be no trifling with her. She was engaged, she told us, to a wrestler – he was in the second order of wrestlers, an 'elephant'. There was only one order above him, a 'lion'. Another, more persuasive, reason for not trifling with her!

She took us some distance outside the town to see the grasslands. They were incredibly beautiful and unforgettable – wide, undulating seas of green, stretching to infinity. One of our party, Frank, an enthusiast for birds, wandered off in search of them, got lost, and when found was severely reprimanded by our guide. The evening was dedicated to a wonderful display of nomadic folk dancing in traditional costume. The Soviets have always encouraged folk art in their satellite states. I was looking forward to hearing old Mongolian deep throat singing. When it came, it was extraordinary. The sound is produced deep in the larynx, throat, stomach and palate, producing two notes and melodies simultaneously, one a low growl and the other an ethereal whistling.

On our last day in that extraordinary land, our guide approached me. Payment was now required for our stay in Mongolia and it must be in American dollars! I promptly explained that everything had been pre-paid by our English agency, payment which included our onward passage by train to

Datong and all our food. Aggressively, she told me that this was not so and that we would not be able to continue our journey unless we paid up at once. I felt very sure of myself. 'Send a fax to our agency and you'll get verification.'

'But we do not have a fax machine!'

'Telephone, then.'

'We can never get through!'

'Put me in touch with the British ambassador.'

'We do not have one.'

On my continuing obduracy, she told me that I would have to face a committee the next morning to explain myself. I returned to the group with the news. They were worried. We were isolated in a communist country, lost to the world and apparently barred from all communication with it. Curiously, I wasn't afraid. Somehow, the knowledge of my British passport fortified me against danger. The next morning, I set out to face the committee, leaving a very worried group behind me, but all of them ready to support me should it be necessary. As I waited in a small bare room to be called, I felt as if I were about to face a committee of the Inquisition. I was summoned into the presence of six or seven unsmiling, hefty women officials, all in some sort of uniform. The interrogation began. I owed them money. How could I expect to have myself and my group housed, fed and entertained without paying for it? I vigorously insisted that everything had been pre-paid by our British agent and that payment had included our ongoing journey to Datong and meals on the train. They aggressively told me that this was not so and that we would certainly not be able to continue our journey unless we paid up at once. The women began to talk among themselves in Mongolian, a language which has been described as 'two cats coughing and spitting at one another until one finally throws up'. Under the circumstances, this increased my fears. After much more of the spitting and coughing, the woman in charge coldly conceded in English that they would provide me with train tickets onward to Datong. 'What about food for the one and a half days' journey?' I asked. More coughing and spitting. She grudgingly conceded that they would give us money to pay for food but that they would expect to be reimbursed in full after we got back to Britain. I was given quite a large amount of paper money and unceremoniously dismissed. I rushed back to the hotel to tell the anxious group what had transpired. 'We won! We've got the train tickets and the money!'

Late that afternoon, we boarded the train for China, installed ourselves in our comfortable bunks and found our way to the restaurant to order our evening meal. I held out my Mongolian togrögs. 'Mongolian money? We do not take Mongolian money. It is worthless. No money, no food!' We had been taken in after all. The 'committee' knew perfectly well that the money was useless and that we would go without dinner that evening. After much coughing and spitting ourselves, we raised enough dollars to go back to the restaurant for food. All that was left was three pots of plum jam and a stale loaf of bread. We chewed the cud of bittersweet reflection along with our plum jam. When we got to the Mongolian-Chinese border, we had to leave the train while the bogies were changed. This took four hours. During that time, the Chinese authorities treated us to a great banquet, washed down with champagne. Speeches of welcome and several toasts were made. This more than made up for being tricked by the Mongolians and made us more than well disposed to the Chinese. But I shall never forget those grasslands.

# Siberia

## 1984

After reading Tolstoy's *Resurrection* I wanted to see Siberia. In that book he describes the life of the convicts sent there under the tsars. Later, the communists were to send their prisoners there too, in much harsher conditions. Dostoevsky and Mandelstam were among the writers who witnessed its horror first hand.

If there is one stretch of the earth which defies imagination, it's Siberia. The mind cannot take in its immensity, its eternal snow and frost, its endless primeval forests, its frozen wastes, its long rivers. Where does such a land begin and end? It stretches from the Ural Mountains in the west to the Pacific in the east and from the Arctic Circle in the north to the Mediterranean in the south. Few have reported from it, or else they weren't heard in the West until Aleksandr Solzhenitsyn wrote *The Gulag Archipelago*, in which he documents the places of exile, forced labour, torture and death of Soviet peoples. Yet the convicts he described were never as 'real' as our own, those of Buchenwald and Auschwitz, whom we could picture and know from the hundreds of television images which passed before us. But Siberian convicts? What did we know of them? Only those who read their accounts could do it. Few images came to us on television.

Yet life in Siberia was more than just gulag civilisation. For centuries, life and trade went on – fishing, hunting and timber for the tribes for whom it was home, the Buryats, the Kalmeks, the Tatars. In 1651, a Cossack army invaded Siberia and brought the tribes to heel, driving them from their lands and handing them over to the tsar. Thus Siberia was opened up to Russia – to Russian traders, missionaries, soldiers and to prisoners, be they criminal, political, undesirable religious communities, men of stubborn national feeling like the Poles and men sent there for no apparent reason at all. This happened under the tsars long before the Soviet regime, when Siberia came to be synonymous with exile. Chekhov, wishing to express his feelings of being exiled in Yalta, where he had removed for health reasons, called it 'my *warm* Siberia'.

But how were these millions of convicts transported across this vast land? The Great Siberian Tract, or Post Road, was developed in the nineteenth century for such transport, with a complex system of holding prisons and exile stations. By 1890, some 34,000 exiles a week were marched in shackles along the Road to Irkutsk; Dostoevsky, Trotsky and Stalin were among the most famous to travel it. In *Resurrection*, Tolstoy describes this never-ending journey from Moscow of prisoners on foot in long lines and the holding stations where they passed the night and thus brought it all before the public consciousness. Dostoevsky, a sentenced convict, made the 2,000-mile journey from Petersburg to Omsk in a closed sledge in freezing temperatures. 'I consider these four years as a time in which I was buried alive and shut up in a coffin,' he wrote. He found all humanity represented in the gulag – criminal, vicious, kindly and even saintly. His book *The House of the Dead* is an account of his experience there. Pasternak's Dr Zhivago spent years in Siberia as a political prisoner. Millions of people – we do not know how many – died there under Stalin's regime. The poet Osip Mandelstam was sentenced to five years in a Siberian gulag for having read out an ironic poem about Stalin which was reported by an informer. It is extraordinary that, in considering what to do with Mandelstam, Stalin telephoned Pasternak, a friend of Mandelstam, in the middle of the night.

'What do you think of Mandelstam's poetry?' asked Stalin. Pasternak, knowing the danger, obfuscated, talking about life and death. Stalin put down the phone. Pasternak always felt guilty about this 'weakness' on his part. Mandelstam's wife documented the whole terrible experience in her fine novels *Hope against Hope* and *Hope Abandoned*. No one knows where Mandelstam was taken, but it's likely that he died in a transit camp on the way to Vladivostok. A fellow convict reports that he had seen him in the gulag clutching a piece of bread.

Chekhov, who was also a doctor, decided to visit and report on the Russian prison colony on the island of Sakalin off the Pacific coast of Russia 'to repay my debt to medicine'. He found atrocious conditions, with prisoners being subjected to the whims of prison governors. On his return, he presented a full report to parliament. All were appalled. Nothing was done. It took Chekhov three months to make the journey from Moscow, often in very harsh weather. Now it was possible for us to make the long journey by train or plane.

To see and experience Siberia – that would be a real adventure! We did the journey from Moscow to Irkutsk by plane so as to avoid the endless flatness of the land journey. Perhaps we were wrong to do so. Beneath us in the darkness, we could see the lights of Omsk and Novosibirsk, new towns where scientists were paid extra to work there. These were places where the cold could kill. As I lay in bed that night in the Intourist Hotel in Irkutsk, I could not take in the fact that in a matter of six hours, I had travelled from Moscow to the heart of the unimaginable land, Siberia. I listened to the sounds from the nearby railway station, the puffing, chortling, whistling of the big engines which were destined for such exotic places as Ulan Bator, Vladivostok, Kamchatka, Beijing. What adventures were possible!

The next day, we visited the busy, bustling city. It was founded in 1651 as a Cossack garrison station in the war against the tribes, becoming rich from trade in fur and ivory. I loved the original wooden houses built snugly to withstand the cold, with their beautiful carved wooden windows. Now, bleak Soviet-style apartment blocks and institutions have killed off the character of this Siberian town. I went in search of the places associated with a group of intellectuals called The Decembrists who had attempted a revolution against the autocratic tsar in December 1825. They bungled the attempt, were caught and either shot or sent into exile in Siberia, leaving behind their families and friends. Prince Volkonsky was one of the most important of these men. For his part in the revolt, he lost control of his estates, his serfs, the medals he had won in the wars against France and was sentenced to twenty years of penal servitude with hard labour, followed by a lifetime of compulsory settlement in Siberia. Maria, his wife, chose to follow him into exile, as did eight other wives of those sentenced. When she saw her husband in shackles, she fell down and kissed his feet. They were later allowed to settle near Irkutsk, and there the story changed.

These aristocrats, who had had serfs to do everything for them in their palaces in Petersburg, now had to learn how to cook, clean, sew, grow vegetables, teach their children and, most extraordinary of all, had to learn Russian in order to communicate with the people, as they had been brought up to speak only French. A real community grew up of people who shared ideas and work

– they developed agriculture, taught native children and discussed philosophy and politics. Volkonsky declared that the Siberian peasant was more dignified and independent than the Russian because he was not a serf. Maria Volkonsky founded schools, a foundling hospital and a theatre. Her husband took to their new life with enthusiasm. 'Manual labour is such a healthy thing,' he wrote to Pushkin, 'and it is a joy when it feeds one's family and is of benefit to other people too.' One year after Maria arrived, her little son died. She never got over this tragedy. One of her fellow exiles was the Princess Trubetskaya, who had also followed her husband, thus also giving up all her hereditary titles and estates. She and three of her children died and are buried in Irkutsk. I found my way to the Church of the Sign in Irkutsk and to the cemetery. I looked on her grave and was shaken to think of all she had gone through – the loss of her family and friends, the loss of her children and her own illness and death. But then, the Princess Trubetskaya who rests here was not the same woman who set out from Moscow in 1826.

When Dostoevsky and his fellow convicts arrived in the holding station of Tobolsk, near Irkutsk, they were met by four of The Decembrists' wives, who presented each of them with a copy of the Gospels. There were ten-rouble notes hidden inside each one of them.

∽

It was almost an hour's journey from Irkutsk to Lake Baikal, the huge, beautiful and mysterious stretch of water we were so anxious to see. I gazed at its blue waters and the high mountains on the other side and thought of all that had happened here. For security reasons, we weren't allowed to go out by boat on its waters, as there were top-secret testing stations there. I gazed and gazed and thought of the tribes who had settled around the mile-long lake, who had worked, fished, hunted and worshipped their gods, totally unaware of what 'developed' society would do to their habitat. The water of that lake, which contains four-fifths of all the fresh water in the world, has been heavily polluted by industry, and its great depth is said to be littered with cars and trucks. The guide over-whelmed us with statistics. The flora and fauna of the lake were unique, and he told us of one curious little fish, the golonskaya, which lives at extreme depths. It's little more than a blob of jelly with a backbone, and when brought to the surface, dissolves into a spot of oil!

We spent four hours in the taiga, the primitive forest which once covered the earth and which I found impossible to imagine. I had expected to see forests of big trees. Instead, I found forests of large, spindly trees which had grown up where the seeds fell at the root. It rained and the paths were wet and muddy. We came to a large wooden hut, our destination for lunch, and could hear singing coming from inside. We went in and took our seats. A German party, from whom the singing came, had already had their lunch and were in high spirits. They paid no attention to us. Riled, we started to sing Irish songs. 'What? Are you Irish? Come and join us!' We all sang 'It's a Long Way to Tipperary' and soon Irish-German relations were toasted in excellent red Siberian wine in the no man's land of the Siberian taiga.

# China: A Holy Mountain

*1984*

We wished to see the modern version of an ancient civilisation which had not long emerged from the Cultural Revolution. Today we are to be pilgrims. We have come especially to this place to go up a holy mountain in order to see the sun rise. High mountains have always inspired people with ideas of holiness, of sainthood, of nearness to God – Croagh Patrick in Ireland attracts thousands of pilgrims every year, as do Mount Sinai and Mount Gilboa in Israel. The ancient Chinese believed that the earth was square and that China itself was square and was bounded on all four corners by holy mountains. Emperors periodically toured these special mountains to view their realm. They were carried up in a sedan chair by slaves and accompanied by a huge retinue of courtiers. Tai Shan on the east coast of the square was the most important of these holy mountains because it was believed that, from here, the sun began its journey westward across the sky. Since ancient times, pilgrims have made the journey up the 5,000-foot steep incline to the summit on foot. They risked finding the peak shrouded in mist and never seeing the sun at all, but they could stay in one of the many monasteries on the way up and meditate on life, death and eternity.

Today it's our turn to make the pilgrimage. We arrive in Tai Shan town at the foot of the holy mountain to find ourselves in the midst of crowds of Chinese. It's a national holiday today and they have come to make the ascent, to picnic, to try out the new cable car which has just been installed by the Japanese and generally to enjoy themselves. The atmosphere is festive and everyone is relaxed and smiling – the one child of the family is carried aloft and photographed over and over again. We deposit our baggage at a hotel in Tai Shan and take only a heavy jersey and a toothbrush with us, as we are to spend the night in a hospice at the summit so that we can be present at dawn to see the great spectacle. It's said in China that if you climb the 600 steps to the top, you will live to be a hundred. I wonder if we who are to go up by mechanical means will qualify? Confucius is said to have made the journey and on reaching the top to have exclaimed, 'The world is small!' while Mao Zedong arrived at the top and cried, 'The East is red!' I wonder what we will find ourselves saying.

Here in this town, Mao's fourth wife, Jing Qing, member of the notorious Gang of Four on whom all Chinese ills are blamed, appeared from nowhere into history in the 1960s only to disappear back into it in 1991 by taking her own life. Today all this suffering is in the past and the people are here to enjoy themselves. Many pilgrims are already climbing up by one of the several main routes, while others are preparing to start.

The Chinese have always had a great feeling for the poetry of nature. I love their stylised landscape painting and the poetic names they give to objects. The entire route to the top is marked by temples, monasteries, pagodas, waterfalls and shrines with lovely names such as Midway Gate to Heaven, Peach Blossom Park, Archway under Heaven, Archway to Immortality, Dragon Spring Nunnery, Azure Cloud Temple and Gate to Heaven.

We are to go up near the top in the new cable car. We can't help feeling that we're cheating the sun. We're taken directly to the boarding platform, where already there is a huge queue of Chinese people waiting to enjoy the new experience. We are very embarrassed at bypassing the other people in this way, but they aren't angry. They wave and smile at us. We crowd into the cabin and then, with a lurch, we are up and out, hanging in the void. A magnificent panorama opens up all around us, peak upon peak, forests, waterfalls, temples, gates marking the route. We have the distinct impression of travelling through a Chinese painting.

We disembark and start the rest of the journey on foot. We pass through several moon-gates, those lovely semi-circular arches into which a half moon would nicely fit, enter temples and add our little mite to the offerings of rice, fruit and nuts which have already been placed there by other pilgrims. At last, we come to our hostel, the Mount

Thai Guest House, where we are to spend the night. It's extremely cold and windy at this height. An official gives out long uhlan coats and Chinese Red Army coats to keep out the cold. We look at each other and laugh to see ourselves thus accoutred and we take photos of each other.

The hostel is simple in the extreme. All beds are in dormitories and the toilets are best avoided. Nobody grumbles. We're like small children on a Sunday school excursion. Our evening meal is taken at a big table in the main room. We sit amongst a small number of foreign tourists and many Chinese. We then try to settle down in our bunks, the rough blankets drawn up to our chins in an attempt to keep out the cold. All is dark. A torch is provided for those unfortunates trying to find the toilets. We are soon asleep.

A loud clanging of a bell awakens us all abruptly. It's pitch dark, but it's time to get up and be ready for the great spectacle. We dress hurriedly in the cold and are ushered out into the darkness by guides and up to the viewing place near the peak. We make out hundreds of dim forms around us who are already in position. All are facing east. The atmosphere is expectant, full of subdued excitement. We look in front of us, straining into the dark. Five minutes pass, then ten, then fifteen. Suddenly a cry goes up! A slender, bright orange disc rises before us out of the darkness. It grows bigger, brighter, more radiant with every second. Entranced, we gaze as we have never gazed before at a sunrise. A great cheer goes up from all of us huddled under our uhlan coats. We remain there, watching, rooted to the spot, reluctant to break this magic moment. The great ball, completed, rises superb, scattering the darkness before it. My lord, the sun has risen. The Chinese smile and make us feel part of this very Chinese event, which is very special, even mystical. Then, as the darkness flees before the sun, tongues are loosened, hands clasped in friendship and all return to the hostel for a hearty breakfast.

# St Patrick's Day in Kathmandu

## 1985

Nepal, a poverty-stricken country sandwiched between India and China, home to Hinduism, birthplace of the Buddha, remained unchanged for centuries.

Nepal had overwhelmed us with its sublime mountains, intoxicating air, temples and people. The hotel in Kathmandu seemed incongruously modern and luxurious in this patently poor country. We were greeted with garlands by the bellboys, the porters and the waiters – all in strict hierarchical order and all in smart, well-made uniforms appropriate to their function. At dinner, a full orchestra was playing, mostly English airs. We had a delicious meal at the end of which the chef appeared to greet us and to ask us where we were from, etc. He had an unmistakably Irish accent. 'Are you from Tipperary?' one of our party asked.

'Yes,' he said, 'how did you know?'

'I'm from Tipperary myself, although I left it some twenty years ago,' came the reply. Tongues wagged. So we were from Northern Ireland. The next day was St Patrick's Day. He said he would make a very special day of it. It wasn't often he had a whole party of Irish in his restaurant.

I complimented him on the excellence of our meal and asked him how he had landed in Kathmandu, coming from Tipperary. 'Oh,' he replied 'finding no work in Ireland, I joined the British Army. I was put into the catering corps and soon discovered that I had a real gift for cooking. I married and my wife and I moved with the army. We soon got tired of constantly moving, so having friends who were British Gurkhas, I asked them to find me a job. They found me a job in this hotel in Kathmandu. The hotel is owned by the king's brother. The royal family own everything here. I had good conditions and my wife was content. Unfortunately, she fell sick some three years ago and died. I don't want to stay here any longer. I now want to return to Ireland. Can any of you help to find me a job?' We all swore we would do what we could to help him, but none of us owned a hotel.

The next day, the restaurant was filled with green flags and the orchestra played Irish airs, including 'It's a Long Way to Tipperary'. A huge birthday cake was wheeled in – it was the saint's birthday and in his honour the white cake was decorated all over with green shamrocks. We had another delicious meal, served by flat-footed Gurkha waiters and a glorious Irish evening flowed over us all, Catholic, Protestant, agnostic, united in a common joy in our country.

On our way out of the restaurant, after excesses of thanks and praise, the chef approached me with a paper in his hand. 'This is my CV. Please send it to hotel managers in Ireland. They will see how extensive my experience has been!' I promised to do so. I glanced over the CV. In large, underlined letters, he had written that his speciality was 'serving cocktails from the back of an elephant while in full chase on a lion hunt'. I laughed aloud as I folded up the paper. This last would be especially appropriate in an Ireland without either cocktails or elephants.

I sent the CV to several hotels, but heard no more of the matter.

# A Chinese Hospital

## 1986

We had seen the northern parts of China and now we were curious to see the southern ones and especially to sail down the gorges of the Yangtze River before a proposed dam flooded the area.

We have arrived at the third of the Three Furnaces of China, at Nanjing. Like Chonquing and Wuhan, Nanjing is a huge industrial city on the Yangtze River with such high temperatures and high humidity in summer that workers are literally living in a furnace. As it's early September, the air has cooled down and we are quite comfortable. We have just completed a journey by boat through the famous Yangtze gorges, gorges with are soon to be flooded by the Chinese and made into a huge reservoir. Our overnight stay in Chonquing, where we went on board the boat, was unlike anything we had yet experienced in China. The old city is literally a mountain which has been squeezed between two rivers. Narrow lanes and broken, steep steps lead from the river up to the town and in every nook and cranny of that old, dirty cliff, it seems that a Chinese family had perched and found a foothold, a makeshift, extremely primitive home. They are like a density of rooks in an old gnarled tree. To embark on the ship the following morning, we had to navigate these cracked steps very carefully, as they were wet and slippery with rain.

We installed ourselves on our river boat, ready for a three-day sail through the famous gorges. Our berths were on the second-class deck reserved for tourists: there was third class, even fourth class below us and those who couldn't afford a berth simply lay on the deck. I saw one man stretched out, fast asleep, with a solitary hen tied to his leg with a piece of string. I was tempted to cut the string and let the bird go free, but I resisted the temptation when I saw that its fate would be no better were it to land on water.

The mountains rose up steep and jagged as if hewn out by an axe above the Yangtze, where the waters swirl and roar as they pass between them. Sometimes the mountains are so steep that we can't even see the sun. In a day's sailing, we arrived at Wuhan and the third day brought us to Nanjing, the third furnace of China. That city suffered terribly from 1931 to 1935 during the Japanese–Chinese War, when the Japanese took this former capital by storm, wantonly killing and looting in an episode known as the Rape of Nanjing. Within a four-day period, approximately 44,000 women were raped and 100,000 Nanjing residents murdered. The end of the war wasn't the end of their sufferings. A civil war followed between the communists under Mao and the nationalists under Ching Kai Shek, in which hundreds of thousands were killed.

The greatest monument in Nanjing, which the Chinese are fiercely proud of, is the Yangtze River Bridge. It's a huge engineering feat, as the engineers were faced with an almost intractable problem – how to erect foundations on bedrock almost seventy feet deep and encased by swirling currents of silt. British and Soviet engineers withdrew from the task in 1960, so the Chinese, with customary ingenuity, did the job themselves. They succeeded in making a two-tier bridge over five thousand feet long for rail and cars. It took almost ten years to complete and seven thousand workers to do the job. It was opened as a triumph of communist China in 1968. No wonder they want to show it off to us. We were taken out by boat out onto the water to admire its lovely lace ironwork, which reminded us of the Eiffel Tower and the Forth Bridge. We eventually came ashore by mounting an iron gangway which led from the boat to the shore.

One of our group, an elderly lady who was partially blind, missed her footing and fell heavily against a painted metal step and cut her leg badly. Blood poured from the wound in an alarming way. Our guide acted promptly. There was a medical centre close by, the Bridge Clinic, from where we could summon aid. What could a medical centre be doing so far from the town and beside a bridge? The answer was a sad one. Some Chinese people, desperate and depressed, tried to commit suicide by throwing themselves off the bridge into the waters beneath. The Bridge Clinic was established to try to rescue them. In a matter of minutes, first-aid personnel arrived and managed to stanch the wound, but advised us to take the patient to the provincial hospital right away because her 'rubber leg' (oedema) ran a grave risk of infection. We must summon an ambulance at once. Could we pay? Were we insured? The ambulance arrived. It was more like an animal cart than transport for humans. It was dirty and bloodstained inside. The patient was laid on a primitive stretcher while myself, her friend and the guide were obliged to sit on chairs which weren't anchored to the floor.

We tore through the streets of Nanjing, holding on tight and praying that we, too, would not be taken, injured, to the hospital. We were deposited in front of a first aid centre. Trolleys were lined up outside. There were no porters – we had to push our patient ourselves to a nearby building where a doctor would see her. After some time, we managed to see a doctor who told us to take the patient on the trolley to another building in the complex. We pushed and shoved the trolley with the frightened patient on board and wondered how we would ever get her attended to.

We managed to get her inside the building, where two male attendants told us to wait while they took her away to see a surgeon. By this time, our patient was very scared. We reassured her that we wouldn't leave her and that we'd be there when the doctor gave his diagnosis. We waited for one hour in a poor, shabby room. The assistants obliged us to put on white gowns 'to avoid infection', but given the state of the place, we feared this measure would be ineffective. Finally, the doctor returned.

'Yes, there is a danger of infection in this lady's leg, infection from the paint and metal she struck. Her leg, because of oedema, is very vulnerable. Her blood pressure is low and she has lost a lot of blood. I shall consult with a surgeon.' We waited for another three hours. What must our patient be thinking? That she had been abandoned? I tried to get a message sent to her by an assistant: 'Tell her that we're still here and won't leave her.' Finally, a young surgeon emerged from a side room. He looked intelligent and capable. He smiled at us. 'Mrs X will need an operation on her leg, and as she has lost a lot of blood, she will need a blood transfusion.'

The words 'blood transfusion' filled me with alarm. Before leaving Belfast, I had sought advice from the medical profession as to what to do should a medical emergency happen to one of us in provincial China. 'Do not take a blood transfusion except in an acute emergency because of the risk of AIDS. If such a transfusion should be absolutely necessary, make sure it's taken from one of your group.' That situation was now upon me! I turned to the smiling surgeon and said, 'I should hate to be in any way disrespectful to your country, but I was warned by the doctors at home not to take a blood transfusion because of the risk of AIDS.' I smiled lamely. His smile broadened. 'Be assured, Madame, that we have no AIDS in China. That pollution comes from the West!' This was a shock. Perhaps he was telling the truth? Perhaps I had been misled? Even more lamely, I said, 'In that case, would you be so kind as to take the blood from one of my group?' I was acutely conscious that I wasn't being very complimentary about Chinese blood. He spoke to the guide in Chinese, then turned to me. 'I am sorry, Madame, but in China we do not take blood from anyone over forty-five years of age.' I was defeated. There was nothing for it – Chinese blood and Chinese operation it must be.

The guide and surgeon conferred again. 'You must pay £1,500 to the hospital before the operation can be carried out.' This was a second shock. We didn't have that much money. I telephoned and faxed her insurance company in London to reply at once. There was no reply. More faxes. No replies. I telephoned her son in London: would he send out the money? He agreed. The insurance company later denied receiving those faxes. I was able to trace every one and prove that they had been sent. Their final avowal was lame indeed: 'they had been misfiled'.

The poor patient was naturally very anxious when she heard that I, as leader of the group, was obliged to leave her in the hospital and continue with our itinerary. To be left behind in a country where she knew no one, couldn't speak the language and was about to be operated on in a 'suspect' hospital mightily alarmed her. I was allowed to go with her into the operation room and stay with her until the operation was about to begin. Her friend who was travelling with her agreed to stay for the five days considered necessary and then to travel on together to Hong Kong to meet up with the group again. I tried to calm myself by remembering how good Chinese medicine was supposed to be, but my heart was in my boots as I said goodbye to her and left her to her fate. She had a Chinese blood transfusion and a Chinese operation. She didn't turn yellow and both transfusion and operation were successful. The group continued to Wuxi, to Suzou, then to Hong Kong. Every evening after dinner in the hotel, our guide, Mr Strang, came to my room and we started the long business of trying to get through to the hospital to find out how our patient was doing. Mr Strang always asked me to put on my TV. In the north of China where he lived, he never saw TV. Many old Hollywood films came on the screen, and when discreet kisses were exchanged between hero and heroine, Mr Strang jumped up and down in great excitement. 'I have never seen kisses before, never before!'

Having reached Hong Kong, I started to prepare for Mrs X's arrival. My instructions were not to let her put her foot to the ground until she reached London. I arranged for a private ambulance to go right inside the airport and up to the plane. A lift would take her from the aircraft and down to the ambulance below. I gave her strict instructions. As I wasn't allowed to accompany the ambulance 'for security reasons', I waited to receive her in the hotel. Imagine my amazement when a taxi, not an ambulance, drew up at the front door and Mrs X and her companion stepped out, walking! They had declined the ambulance and preferred the taxi. She survived that experience too.

# Sky High Over Africa

## *1990*

Kenya and Tanzania have fully answered our expectations with their magnificent wild animals and their exotic tribes.

It is eleven o'clock at night and I have settled myself into a window seat of a KLM aeroplane. We are 30,000 feet above Africa, where I have just spent three weeks. We are bound for Amsterdam and then onward to our separate destinations. I love these long night flights in the indigo blue blackness outside the cabin window, where the stars shine with a brilliance that we don't see at home. I know I will find it nearly impossible to sleep, for my head is bursting with all the impressions, sights, sounds and smells which have assailed me on this, my first visit to Africa. As drinks are dispensed by the hostess, I become aware of my neighbour, a tall, distinguished-looking man of about seventy. He looks quietly ahead of him as he sips a large vodka. As we are going to be neighbours for many hours, I attempt a conversation. To my surprise, he is not averse to it. I learn that he's a Dane and that he has lived and worked as an engineer in Tanzania for many years. He is on his way back for a short break to his native country. A few courtesies follow.

After a while, he says quite calmly, as if it were the most natural thing the world, 'We shall never meet again. We can talk.' I listen attentively. 'I have been living with a woman in Tanzania for ten years now, a black woman, forty-three years old, educated, a professional woman. She has given me a son, an African son, Peter. He is now seven years of age, the child of my old age, an Absalom for me. Of course, I have a family in Denmark, all grown up now. Some of them live in Paris.' He remains quiet for a while, as his mind dwells on his Danish family.

'What do they think of their father's long stay in Africa?' I ask. 'And of their African brother?'

'They do not like their father doing these things, having an African mistress and an African son. They want me to turn my back on Africa and come home. But I love this beautiful country of Africa. My heart is there. And I love Peter. A year ago I took him to Denmark to see if I could make a Dane of him. He is quick and intelligent. But where is the boy's home? I must be sure of that, for I shall soon be gone and what will the boy do without me? It seems to me that his home is with his mother, in Africa. But Africa is a maddening country, inefficiency and corruption everywhere, and I, a Dane, have been used to an organised society. I want to give the boy a chance to do well and honestly. I am going now to Denmark to give myself a respite, to come to some sort of decision. I have to be very careful what I say in both countries because I am constantly accused of being racist.'

He pours himself another drink. 'If anyone had told me that I was going to have such a conversation on a plane with a complete stranger ... I have never talked of these things before. I am, by nature, a reserved Dane.' I can see that he is nervous about his forthcoming reception by his Danish family; he is the prodigal father going home to his sons. 'The trouble is, I love my Danish children. Where now am I to end my days? I asked Peter's mother if she would care for me and at the end put me in a box and bury me decently. I have not yet had an answer. I am going now to see what that, my final situation, might be in Denmark.' He looks quietly and calmly ahead of him, totally absorbed. 'How good it is to talk. In Africa I have the problem of language. I have never been able to say these things I am saying to you now. The questions you ask!'

Only once do I speak of myself, telling him briefly of my own relationship with my father. I tell him how I had looked after him, a difficult and independent man, in his final years, more out of duty than anything else. 'If only he had been able to speak to me directly of his feelings, for he certainly loved me. If he could have broken through the impersonal tones of a lifetime, I would have understood, would have forgiven him his hard ways with me and a flood of tenderness would have flowed out towards him. But a lifetime's habits were too hard to break. He was still the father and I the child.' I can see that he sees the application to himself, for there are tears in his eyes. 'Perhaps you should stop being the father and just be the man. It would be easier for everyone.'

A long silence follows. Then, 'Since we are talking like this, I must tell you that I have had an affair with a third woman and have a daughter by her in Denmark. And, do you know, a strange thing … she is studying theology and is going to be a priest of the church! I shall talk theology with her and try to understand. I am not a church-goer, but when I look at the wonders of the earth, I know there must be a creator. I want to think about that more and more now that I am an old man, an old man looking back at my own parents, farmers who lived a life of hard work and died in their nineties with the same dignity as they had lived. That is the only way.' He remains silent for a while, internally absorbed, then continues, 'I wish I had looked after my first wife better. She died a year ago. That would not have happened in Africa. They look after each other there.'

'Four daughters,' I say. 'You must read Shakespeare's *King Lear*. That's about a father and a daughter, an old man, too. It is the grace of the daughter's love which saves that troubled and troubling father. Grace is a religious term, I know, but it's the most beautiful word in our language.'

'You have read a lot of books?' he asked.

'Yes, it's my profession and also my passion.

Tolstoy, now – you would love his books. He, too, became old, full of thought and trouble and trying to understand, just like you.'

At 4.30 a.m. they wake everyone for breakfast. Quietly, we resume our conversation. 'Denmark – you belong to a race that has always had initiative. The Africans aren't the same, but perhaps there are qualities more important than initiative?'

'Yes, it is true,' he says, 'but it is best not to mix the cultures. It is too much of a strain on the personality.' I tell him of my cousin who married an African academic in Nigeria. She had one child. Eventually the marriage broke up. She returned with her daughter to live in London. The daughter was able to get a good English education and is now a GP. But she isn't happy. She doesn't know where she belongs. Her mother now believes that she has done her wrong by removing her from her African culture. He perfectly understands. I sense his longing to continue talking, to probe his situation at a slow, meditative pace, but the imminent landing at Amsterdam has already been announced.

As the plane lands, I turn to him and offer my hand. For the first time he looks directly into my eyes. 'Thank you. I shall not forget our conversation.'

I shake his hand. 'May all go well with you in Denmark.'

# Iran

## 1996

Iran was once the home of the mighty Persian Empire which had defeated the Greeks and was then defeated in its turn. Although rarely visited, it has an immense cultural heritage, including the remains of Persepolis and the cities of Shiraz and Isfahan. It is the country of the poet Omar Khayyam, whose poems are well known through the translations of Edward Fitzgerald.

The countries of the Middle East are so bound up in each other's history, religions and culture and have undergone such similar invasions and revolutions that to see one part of it is to invite you to see another. Constantinople and the Byzantine Empire, followed by the Turkish Empire, had been our first initiation into that melting pot that is Asia. Turkey, Jordan, Syria and Central Asia were now to be followed by Iran.

Iran didn't sound inviting to the ordinary Western tourist. Here was an Islamic republic, a dictatorship, in fact, with a secret police whose recent record on human rights was not strong, a country where all women in public places had to be covered from head to toe by the dictates of men. It hadn't been long since the Islamic Revolution of 1978, when the handsome, charming Shah whose glamour attracted women the world over was overthrown. Under Western influence, the Shah's reign began well – he brought in many reforms, including doing away with the obligatory wearing of the chador for women. Many women were scandalised, preferring to stay indoors than go outside 'naked'. He was going too fast. The discovery of oil in 1974 brought, as it usually does, both wealth and troubles. Under America's business influence, the Shah spent millions on useless arms. Galloping inflation meant that the rich became richer and the poor, poorer. The economy failed in the late 1970s and there were bloody confrontations between the Shah and the opposition. Finally, he had to flee the country and was harried from one country to another before finally settling and dying in Egypt in 1980.

Ayatollah Khomeini returned to Iran from France in 1979 and the Islamic Republic of Iran was born. It was extremely opposed to everything American, 'The Great Satan'. In 1989, Khomeini died and Rafsanjani was elected President. He did his best to normalise relations with the outside world. During the Kuwait War, Iran under Rafsanjani observed strict neutrality, thus giving themselves credit with the West. Iran began to open its doors to tourists, though few people profited from this. If there were few or no tourists, we told ourselves, we would be doubly welcome. We were right.

❧

To see modern Iran, with all its strengths and weaknesses, was exciting. To see Persia was another thing (Iran is the older name of the country). At school, we learned of the Persian Empire, of how the Persians threatened the Greeks and were beaten by them at Marathon. All us children were on the side of the Greeks because our writers and historians felt much closer to Greek culture than Persian. Persia, like most of Asia, was invaded time and time again by Arabs, Turks, Genghis Khan and Tamburlaine, yet they kept their identity and their culture. We had all heard of Persian miniature paintings, of Persian carpets, Persian writers, great cities like Shiraz and Isfahan and the extraordinary remains of Persepolis, among other remarkable ruins. We would go and see for ourselves.

We, too, would have to obey the dictates of the mullahs and cover up from head to toe once we got outside the bedroom door of the hotel. Some women refused to join us for this reason, but the rest of us found it exciting to have to act in an Islamic play for a few weeks. We bought long dresses, trousers and ample blouses, for no part of the anatomy could be hinted at by too tight a fitting. We bought or made big headscarves which covered our head, neck and shoulders. I rather fancied myself in my large white one.

En route to Teheran, we came down in Damascus. As we neared the airport, we saw what we took to be a field of large white flowers beneath us. As we descended further, we saw that these 'flowers' were in fact a mass of plastic bags which had been drawn in here by the suction of the airplane engines! Damascus had joined the twentieth century. As we descended towards Teheran Airport, we put on our headscarves and checked our skirts and trousers. We were going on stage! We looked at each other and laughed. We were ready for fun. The customs inspectors were slow and sour, saying, 'You must have patience.' We were shown into special cabinets where body searches were performed by female Islamic guards. My woman glared at me, pointed to my forehead and shouted 'Hejab! Hejab!', pulling my scarf roughly further over my forehead. This was my first encounter with that rough army of men and women who were recruited to see that Islamic law was enforced everywhere. We were soon to discover that ordinary Iranians did not like the guards and even the government found it hard to keep them in check. For the moment, the whole country was in the grip of Islamic law, although our guide was later to tell us that 'freedom' was practised behind closed doors and with money you could do what you liked.

After dinner that first evening, the clouds rolled away to reveal big snow-covered mountains enclosing Teheran in a huge bowl. There are nine million people living in the city, mostly in apartment blocks. It is a stony, bony landscape for those of us used to greenery and gardens, but we were told that both trees and gardens were being planned for the city.

The next day, well enveloped, Sam, our guide,
took us to see one of the glories of modern Iran,
the huge but unfinished mosque dedicated to Ayatollah Khomeini, about twenty miles from the
capital. The frenzy of devotion manifested to
imams past and present is amazing. They seem to
elicit even more fervour than the saints of Christianity. The mosque was immense, bigger than two
or three football pitches. Some people were praying, others simply picnicking on the ground with
their children, teachers even leading children by
the hand from point to point. The whole atmosphere was happy and relaxed. Everyone was fascinated by us foreigners in our queer clothes. We
greeted them in English and smiled. They answered, 'Welcome to Iran! Welcome to Iran!' and
that was the happy extent of their vocabulary. Beside this huge mosque was a large and very sad
cemetery where the thousands of young soldiers
who were slaughtered in the Iran–Iraq War of
1980–88 are buried, in which the West backed Sad-
dam and Iraq. Each tombstone carried a photo of
the dead soldier and on many of these graves
mothers and wives sat weeping, remembering a
war that most of the rest of the world has forgotten.

Today, we are flying to the north-east of Iran, to
Mashad, in that wild part which borders on
Afghanistan, to pay our respects to another imam,
the famous Imam Reza, a direct descendent of Ali,

son-in-law of the Prophet. Those who claim this
line are called Shi-ites, while those who claim descent from an elected caliph are called Sunnis.
These two branches of Islam look with great suspicion on one another. Only in Iran do Shi-ite
Muslims form a majority of the population. We
can tell that this is an important place of pilgrimage from the crowds who are making their way
down every road to the holy shrine. All are excited
and eager. The whole mosque complex, unlike
Mecca and Medina, is open to non-Muslims, except for the holy shrine itself. We are again taken
aside, clad in black chadors, and conducted into
the mosque where other imams are buried. We are
caught up in another frenzy of devotion. Heavily
veiled women caress and kiss the latticed cages enclosing the tombs. Weeping, they kiss the locks,
hinges and framework and invite us to do the
same. Rather than offend the faithful, I press my
lips to places where other lips have been pressed
and hope for the best.

The curator of the adjacent museum is waiting
for our 'delegation'. It's a magnificent museum
where beautiful objects, often donated by pilgrims,
are on display. He spares us no detail in our two-
hour visit. I try to look as if I understand it all.

The afternoon is to be dedicated to poetry.
Near Mashad, several famous Persian poets have
lived and written and we, as a literary group, are
expected to appreciate them. We visit the mausoleum of Ferdusi, a very famous poet. We know

nothing about him, but manage to conceal our ignorance. Our guide recites some of his verses in Persian. We clap enthusiastically. Next comes a poet we *have* heard of, Omar Khayyam, better known in Iran as an astronomer and mathematician. We know his verses thanks to the translations into English of Edward Fitzgerald. The guide again recites his verses in Persian. This time, we can recite some of them in English, to the great surprise of our audience, which is getting bigger by the minute.

Suddenly, a beautiful sound, like a note on a perfect musical instrument, breaks the silence. It's the sound of an old man singing a sad, spiritual melody. There was no need for translation. The crowd is entranced. The old man is a beggar and holds out his hat.

The guide explains to the crowd who we are and where we come from. Many of them don't know where Ireland is. Without invitation or warning, Doreen from our group starts to sing a lovely old Irish melody in a light, controlled voice. The crowd is entranced and wants more! She sings two or three other airs. The warmth of the reception is sweet. We feel as if an Irish–Iranian pact of friendship has just been sealed by poetry and music.

The mausoleum of a mystic poet, Attar, follows. We board the bus to return to Mashad. We look out at the huge scale of this landscape of mountain and desert. It's raining. Suddenly, the bus comes to a halt and two Islamic guards get on.

This is not unusual, as they regularly check vehicles. Unsmiling, they look at our passports. The guide and driver are in earnest conversation with the two men, a conversation which is becoming more and more heated. The guide tells us that the guards are demanding $5 from each of us to allow us to continue on our way. This is one of the ways of making money for themselves. I say that in no circumstances will we pay and the guide agrees. Driver, guide and guards get off the bus and the argument continues outside. We watch, intrigued. They now want the driver to pay. Did he pay? I suspect so. His company would be anxious to keep tourists happy, whatever the cost. Eventually, the driver and guide get on again and we are on our way. The guide has taken a note of the number of the car.

When we arrive back in Mashad, we're taken to a very special local restaurant. It's like something out of Arabian Nights. Walls of glass are decorated all over with coloured lights and artificial flowers – what we would call 'high vulgar' fashion! That evening, a representative from our tour company comes to see me about the 'incident' on the bus. 'You must not be afraid, Mrs Devlin!'

I replied in all sincerity, 'But we were never afraid!'

From the windswept northern corner of Iran, we were next transported to Kerman in the warm south. We are here to visit the famous site of Bam, a medieval town in the desert made entirely from mud and straw and abandoned nearly two hundred years ago. We drive 110 miles through a wide, barren desert landscape to get to Bam. It's getting hotter and hotter and when we get out of the bus at Bam, it's over 100 degrees Fahrenheit and we are to explore the city on foot in the heat.

How complete is the whole city! The encircling walls of mud are still so intact that there is only the one original narrow entrance to the city. The turrets at the top of the city tell us that this was a military town which had to defend itself. Beneath the fortifications is a whole town of streets, bazaars, mosques and houses. Life and business went on here apace. There is now silence and nothingness. The government want to preserve this extraordinary city and will use it for 'architectural studies'. Bam is famous for dates and I, who love dates, am sad to learn that the season is over.

Hot and tired, we emerged from Bam to find that Sam had reserved seats for us outside a restaurant at long tables in the shade. We were surprised to see some German and French tourists already seated. We were the last to arrive but the first to be served because Sam, seeing that the staff were overwhelmed, just went into the kitchens and served us himself. We had a delicious aubergine stew with nuggets of meat and a salad of tasty tomatoes and lettuce.

We hadn't expected to see lovely gardens anywhere in Iran because water is scarce in this desert part of the earth. We were wrong. We saw many classical gardens very different from our cottage gardens and green lawns but still very beautiful in themselves. We were now on our way to see one near Kerman, known as the Governor's Garden. In the middle of this desert land, the designer had made an architectural garden of stone, greenery and water. It is stepped geometrically, with a lovely fall of fountains and green shrubs within a rectangle. There is little colour – all is strong, severe, even spiritual. After seeing four or five of these gardens in Iran, I came to admire and enjoy their cool symmetry in the same way I admired the bare ribbed structure of the domes in Samarkand, shorn by time of their tiles and decorations.

A long drive through huge landscapes on a scale we are quite unaccustomed to in the West brought us to Shiraz, 'city of nightingales and roses'. On our way, Sam found a cool little plateau beside a stream where, for lunch, he dispensed yards of fresh naan bread, goats' cheese, tomatoes and olives. A lorry drew up nearby and two men got out, pulled out pipes and began to smoke opium. I was intrigued. I had read a good deal about the effects of opium on Coleridge and De Quincy. I drew near the men. They offered me a pipe and with a certain feeling of trepidation I took a long, deep breath right into my lungs. I waited. Nothing happened!

By this time, our bus driver had become very friendly and, within the limits of his vocabulary, he tried to tell us about Iran. When he thought it was safe to do so, he would shout 'Scarves off!' and we would take them off gratefully. When he saw Islamic guards on the road in front, he would shout 'Scarves on!' and we would be nicely enveloped when the guards got on the bus and inspected us. It was my firm impression that ordinary Iranian people had no time for the excesses of the guards, but there was nothing they could do about it.

In Shiraz, a group of women university students descended on us in their black chadors. We seemed to be in an immense convent. 'How do you like Iran?' they asked.

'Very much, very much indeed!'

'Well, we don't! We do not like having to wear these chadors. We cannot sit beside boys in class nor eat with them and we have nothing to do in the evenings!'

'Where are you from?' they then asked. 'Can I write to you? Give me your address.' In spite of giving my address over and over again, I never received a single letter from Iran. Were they afraid?

In Shiraz, Sam made us wait until after dinner before visiting its famous mosque. We soon knew why. The brilliantly tiled dome and the two gold minarets were then reflected faithfully in the long rectangle of water especially built for that purpose. It was an unforgettable sight. A new moon in the bare dark sky above added to the sublime beauty of the whole. Shiraz was one of the greatest cities of the Islamic world when this mosque was built in the thirteenth century. It was the leading centre for calligraphy, painting, architecture and literature. To go inside the mosque, we had again to be clad in chadors, white this time, which made us look like a band of angels. The interior was astonishing. Vast numbers of minute mirror tiles, both flat and angled and of extraordinary intricacy, made the whole space dazzle with light. Locks and hinges on the tombs were all of silver. Men and women prostrated themselves in a frenzy of devotion and invited us by gestures to do likewise. I was 'commanded' to kiss the casing of one of the tombs, to caress it as she was doing. It was very difficult to keep from hysterical laughter. Elma is on the floor in a heap of what appears to be heaving emotion, when in fact, under her chador, she is in hysterics. The head of the local Islamic guards is here. Some tourists complained yesterday that the Islamic guards were very aggressive towards them. He knows this is bad for tourism. He is here to restrain their petty bullying.

If there is a high point in this country of high points, it has to be Persepolis. It was the capital of the great Persian Empire in the sixth century BC, the biggest empire the world had ever seen. I first heard of Persepolis when studying Marlowe's *Tamburlaine* at Trinity. Marlowe's imagination was set on fire by the story of Tamburlaine the Terrible, the Mongol whose ambition to conquer the world was limitless:

*Is it not passing brave to be a king*
*And ride in triumph through Persepolis?*

And now here I was, walking where kings had walked – Cyrus, Darius the Great, Xerxes, Alexander the Great, Genghis Khan and Tamburlaine. In 331 BC, Alexander the Great 'accidentally' burnt Persepolis to the ground, but not before he had its enormous library translated into Greek! Here were enormous palace complexes set in this wide plain. Here prisoners were brought, tribute paid, victories celebrated. Part of the Great Stairway still remains and we mount the steps and admire the stylised reliefs on the side, captors and captured. The seven-metre-high stone bulls are on a scale I have never seen before. The local guide brought us to part of the palace from where the Emperor watched the lions playing in the den in front of him. Could this possibly be where Daniel was thrown?

Below the ancient city, we saw the remains of a tent city which the Shah had assembled in 1971 to celebrate the 2,500th anniversary of the Persian Empire. The Shah attended with a glittering array of international royalty and dignitaries. It was to be his swan song.

The next day, on our way to Isfahan, we stopped for a short break in the countryside and saw an amazing sight. As we were wandering about, we heard the sound of horses' hooves behind us. We had just enough time to jump out of the way before a procession of horses briskly crossed our path. It was a whole community of Kurdish nomads on the move. At the front of the procession rode the leader, a dark, masterful, swarthy man who could easily have been cast as Rochester in *Jane Eyre*. He set the pace, which was quick and purposeful. Behind him rode the men on horses or donkeys, then the women, their brilliant coloured skirts spread out on the animals' backs behind them like great peacock tails. Their heads were uncovered, as is permissible for Kurdish women. Then came their possessions, folded tents, skins, pots and pans, bags, all tied onto donkeys. Then came the most extraordinary sight of all, their animals perched on the back of donkeys – a clutch of chickens in a cloth riding on one, a bag of newborn lambs on another, a magnificent cock standing proudly upright on another and keeping steady with the motion, a puppy sitting up straight on a moving back. Dogs walked by the side of the procession, strong and disciplined. All kept up a good pace, reining in the horses when necessary and keeping close, one behind the other. They don't like us tourists gazing at them and they show their displeasure when they hear the cameras click. I marvel at this sight, at the strict hierarchy of man and beast, where each knows his place and keeps it and where authority is not questioned. Democrat though I am, I suddenly feel nostalgic.

It's worth travelling to Iran just to see the city
of Isfahan, which houses the greatest concentration of beautiful Islamic monuments in Iran. Shah
Abbas in the sixteenth century set out to make Isfahan a great and beautiful capital city. It is all of
a piece, one exquisite harmony of architecture,
shapes and spaces, of gardens and bazaars, of river
and bridges. We look in wonder at the Meidun-e-
Eman, the huge open square with its magnificent
mosque, portal and minaret. Inside and out it is
covered by pale blue tiles, the 'blue of Isfahan', and
at whatever angle you look at it, the colour subtly
changes, never losing its glorious sheen. After the
Taj Mahal, the mosque Masjed-ē-shah, at one end
of the square, must be one of the most sublime
buildings in the world. Here, tile and colour and
design reach the apotheosis of sheer beauty.
Everyone in Isfahan seemed very relaxed. There
was no fever of devotion, no excessive clamour in
the bazaar. And there were virtually no tourists. We
had all this beauty to ourselves.

Back in Teheran, we are nearing the end of our
visit and I am anxious to find some old Persian
tiles. Sam leads me through narrow streets until we
come to an old rickety shop which sells bits and
pieces of plaster and building material. The old
man behind the counter points out an old box full
of pieces of tiles and plaster. I rummage among
them and find four or five tiles complete. They are
very old, hand made, and they depict in a most

lively fashion a woman weaving, a man fishing and other everyday activities. They cost very little. I love them. I went into a carpet shop and bought a rug. As I had promised myself not to be tempted by yet another rug, I will say no more and give no details!

# Pakistan: The Roof of the World

## 1997

We wanted to go to Pakistan to see the recently opened Karakoram Highway which links Pakistan to China by perilous mountain passes which cross valleys whose inhabitants had known nothing of the outside world until the highway was made.

It was in a small hotel perched right above the mighty river Indus in the high mountains of Pakistan that Qumar told me his extraordinary story. But first, let me take you there.

When you have been on the roof of the world, as I have been, you are never quite the same again. Whether it was Tibet or the Himalayas or the Andes, your mind permanently changes direction – it's stretched vertically and vertiginously and you're no longer sure where your control compass is. This happened to me in Pakistan. The image of Pakistan in the minds of many Europeans is unattractive. The name suggests teeming cities, dirt, disease, poverty, heat and an overdose of Islamic fervour, a place to be avoided rather than sought out. We hadn't intended to visit Pakistan, having the same image of that country as our fellow Europeans. The exquisite lakes and mountains of Kashmir were in our sights, but it soon became impossible to contemplate a visit there because of the political situation. After India became independent from Great Britain in 1947, that part of India we now call Pakistan became independent of India. Partition was rough justice, as it always is, and feelings ran very high between the two parts of the subcontinent, for India was largely Hindu and Pakistan was largely Muslim. These impassioned feelings reach boiling point from time to time over the disputed territory of Kashmir, which has a Muslim majority but which belongs to India – a poisonous and infallible recipe for trouble. China, Pakistan and India patrol its icy borders and keep an iron eye on each other. Kashmir was out for tourists, but there was Pakistan, and it turned out to be an even more interesting place.

The whole northern area of Pakistan is unknown to all but the most intrepid and curious travellers, as it's dense with huge mountain ranges that have been well nigh impenetrable for centuries. The Himalayas, the Karakorams and the Hindu Kush ranges are inhospitable to man. Only caravans of hardy yaks and camels made the 1,200-kilometre journey from China to India over these mountains – and that on a mere donkey track, a journey that took three months. For these caravans and their traders, it meant crossing wild mountain passes and valleys where little tribal kingdoms had lived for centuries cut off from each other and from the outside world. They lived by their own codes, their own tribal laws and dispensed their own justice. Then everything changed.

China and Pakistan decided to link their two countries by a road which would go from Sinkiang in China to Islamabad in Pakistan. This road would have a political as well as a commercial use. The idea, said to be the Aga Khan's, was huge and ambitious. They would do it together. China blasted the way from her side and Pakistan from hers. It was begun in 1964 and it took twenty years to complete what has been called 'the greatest engineering feat since the building of the Pyramids'. The road was hacked out of the rock face – it crossed glaciers, narrow mountain passes, swollen rivers and precipitous gullies, and all at frozen altitudes. Four hundred bridges were constructed, those on the Pakistani side to Pakistani design and those on the Chinese side to Chinese design. The working conditions were certainly horrific, dangerous and poorly paid; more than four hundred men were killed during the construction, mostly by dynamite. This road is known as the Karakoram Highway (KKH) because it crosses the Karakoram mountain range. It was declared complete only in 1975, and only in 1986 was it opened all the way to China. Maintenance of such a road is an extremely difficult task at all times, as the mountains are always threatening to take back what is rightly theirs with rock falls and earthquakes, mud and scree floods. It is the business of the Pakistani army to

maintain this highway. The great River Indus forms
the backbone of the whole terrain – it has carved
out for itself a tempestuous bed, starting in the
high Tibetan plateau, crossing the Karakoram
range in deep valleys and gullies and gorges, then
on down to the parched plains of the Punjab before emptying itself into the Arabian Sea. To see
such a river would in itself be worth the journey.
Such a journey was not for faint hearts, but I had no
difficulty in getting nineteen women and one husband to sign up for it! Single women, always intrepid travellers, and married women, some in the
easiest of circumstances, left their husbands at
home and signed on. It promised to be a great adventure. And it was.

We flew direct from London to Lahore by Pakistani
Airlines. The plane was full to bursting with Pakistani
businessmen, Pakistani people going home to visit relatives, Pakistani children and Pakistani babies, all with
Pakistani luggage, parcels and plastic bags up on the
racks, under the seat, on laps – everywhere. My Pakistani neighbour was puzzled. Why did so many women
from Ireland wish to visit his country? He wasn't
thinking of the Karakoram Highway, but of the
crowded cities. 'You are flying to Peshawar? How
unusual! I hope your plane arrives safely. You know
what Pakistanis call PIA [Pakistani International
Airlines]? Please Inform Allah! Pain in the Arse!
Panic in the Air! May Allah go with you!' I liked his
sense of humour – it boded well.

At Lahore Airport, immense crowds of people were pushing against the barrier, looking out for friends and relatives, many carrying bunches of flowers as greetings. Like a miracle, in the midst of this throbbing mass, an agent sent to meet us found us at once. Outside the terminal, our bus was waiting. Fantastic traffic chaos and milling crowds pressed on all sides. We were in the Sub-Continent! That afternoon, we had a quick look at Lahore, at its fort and its famous Shalimar Gardens, and we had tea under the banyan tree. We stayed in great luxury at the Pearl Continental Hotel. We were greeted with garlands of flowers and invited to welcome drinks in the foyer. As tour leader, I've always been treated with great attention when a tip was expected. Here, it exceeded all attentions anywhere! My glass of fruit juice was held for me by a waiter standing to attention at my side, and every time I wanted a sip, I had to signal to him; he then raised the glass to my lips, allowed me a sip, then solemnly returned the glass to his hand and stood at attention until I should signal for another one. It was most uncomfortable and embarrassing.

The next morning, we were up at six and ready for our flight to Peshawar and the start of our journey. We emerged from the plane into the terminal building among another bewildering crowd of people. A young, handsome Pakistani man stepped forward to greet us, having had no difficulty in recognising nineteen mature women from the British Isles! He was called Qumar and was to be our guide for the whole journey. Tourists were scarce. He'd had no group for the past five months. Trouble in Kashmir and Afghanistan had frightened people, but there was no need. He promised us a wonderful journey on the KKH. (That highway, which we had never even heard of before preparing for our trip to Pakistan, was now familiarly known to us by its initials.) We would be entirely in his hands and in the capable hands of the two drivers of the minivans which were to convey us. He then introduced Heider, the senior driver, and Majeed, the junior one. Qumar said they were experienced mountain drivers and our safety would be assured on the perilous journey which lay ahead. As tour leader, I was placed in Heider's van.

The next morning was given over to a quick view of Peshawar. It was choked with tongas, rickshaws, motorbikes, bicycles, bullock carts, sheep, goats and women gliding about in black burkas at the market. All seemed in total disorder. The streets were crowded with men, most of them in the long brown garment which they wear so well and the flat Pakistani cap with a brim which sticks out around the head like a saucer, while others wore brilliantly coloured turbans. They gesticulated, laughed, bargained and drank tea. Street stalls spilled out fruits of all kinds, vegetables, spices and grains in delicious array. Small shops glittered brilliantly with copper and brass. This, then, was the capital of the North-West Frontier Province, a wild and woolly cowboy country, home of the famous Pathan tribesmen. They are tall, muscular men with fine features, famed for their fighting prowess and for their fierce tribal codes of honour. The turban, made of yards of material, can be unwrapped to serve as a shroud should they die fighting for their cause. For centuries, the North-West Frontier between Afghanistan and India (now Pakistan) has been such a wild and lawless place that the Pakistani government, like the British before them, have shut their eyes to what goes on, allowing the Pathans to govern themselves in return for some concessions.

That afternoon, the big question was on everyone's lips: 'Can we do the Khyber Pass?' Every schoolboy has heard stories of this famous Pass, which joins Pakistan and Afghanistan – of the famous armies that have passed along it and the fights that have gone on there. It is a notoriously sensitive area, heavily guarded by the military and more often than not barred to tourists. Since the Soviet invasion of Afghanistan in 1979 and the subsequent reign of the barbaric Taliban, millions of refugees have swarmed through the Pass from Afghanistan, settling illegally along it and making their living by smuggling. There are now 4.5 million refugees in Pakistan, a huge problem for the government. We learned that no permission had been granted to use the Pass for the past two years. 'It all depends on the political situation,' said

Qumar. 'I will go to the political agent's office and see what can be done.' He took us to the museum and left us there while he did the business.

The museum was a great surprise. It exhibited many items of Gandharan art, a beautiful, unusual art we'd never heard of before. Its inspiration, colours, designs and shapes come from the mingling of two ancient cultures in the North-West Province, the Buddhist culture and the Greek culture that arrived with the conquests of Alexander the Great. I loved it all, especially the life-sized stylised wooden figures of Alexander the Great's soldiers on horseback from the third century BC. They were complete and striking.

While we were admiring some lovely Gandharan jewellery, Qumar burst in to tell us the amazing news. We had been given permission to 'do' the Khyber! We had to leave at once in case there was a change of mind or of the political situation. We were quickly stowed into our minivans and were on our way. On the edge of the town, we were stopped at a military post. Two men in black uniforms with Kalashnikovs boarded our vans and examined our permits. The soldiers were young, stern and unshaven in the Islamic style. They were decidedly uncomfortable in the presence of so many uncovered, unaccompanied women; women in Pakistan were firmly discouraged from such wanderings. We knew that these men wanted to know where our husbands were, for it was unthinkable in Pakistan for women of our age not to be married. Another lean, sinewy soldier in black boarded our vans and examined our passports, carefully avoiding all eye contact. We knew better than to try to engage him in light conversation. Satisfied at last, he sat down on the front of the van and nursed his Kalashnikov between his knees and off we went, now completely in the hands of the Pathan tribesmen where Pakistani law did not obtain.

We bumped along a very uneven road, with myself in the vulnerable position over the wheel. We were all extremely alert and excited. We soon came to a great stone arch called the Khyber Gate, which marks the official entrance to the Pass. Again, we were stopped by armed men in black and again our passports were examined with no eye contact. We felt like felons and were very still and quiet, quite unlike ourselves. Then we were through the Gate and into the Pass where Alexander had passed with his army, as had Genghis Khan and Tamburlaine after him. Our road zigzagged for miles, now broad, now narrow. The scenes which met our eyes were extraordinary.

Colonies of refugees had established themselves in tents and makeshift huts on both sides of the road in an ingenious and tenacious effort to reconstruct their lives. Stalls of smuggled goods lined the roadside – guns, rifles, bullets, hashish, cocaine, opium, TVs and radios and even Marks & Spencer T-shirts. Brightly decorated lorries

crunched by on their way to and from
Afghanistan. We learned that there was a strike in
Afghanistan against high flour prices and that Pakistanis were taking their own flour to sell at higher
prices there than they could get at home. Angry
young men were trying to jump on the lorries to
pull off sacks of flour. Fleets of bicycles laden
with goods back and front were being pedalled furiously by young men, their long brown garments
billowing out behind them. They hired bicycles
from local entrepreneurs and made the eleven-mile
journey up and down the Pass with smuggled
goods.

The rock wall along the Pass was riven from
time to time by a series of narrow passes topped
by forts from whose menacing gun-slits the
Pathans would have pounded the enemy below.
Wall plaques on the rocks commemorated the
Khyber's turbulent history and its past glories. A
huge rock was inscribed with the names and insignia of British regiments which had served there.
There could hardly have been a British regiment
which did not at some time or another serve in
India. (I thought of my mother's sister from West
Cork. She had married a soldier in the British
Army and had gone out to India with him. She
came home by ship to have her first baby. The
birth happened prematurely and both mother and
baby died and were buried at sea.)

Awed by the rugged landscape and the press of
history, we watched silently. Our vans came to a

stop at Londi Kotol and we knew we were nearing the border. More scrutinising of our passports. In another few miles, we were at Torkham, the last checkpoint on the Pass. We got out of our vans and looked, spellbound, into the wild landscape that was Afghanistan, land of revolution and terror, of the notorious Taliban, which had closed the country to all tourists. I was to look into Afghanistan some years later from Iran, when it was still impossible to visit it.

The next day was the start of our big adventure. Our luggage was lifted onto the roof of the vans and tied down securely. We passed through the bustling street of Peshawar and out into the countryside on the first leg of our journey. I sat just behind Heider. He looked worn and tired. I asked him about himself and his work. 'How old do you think I am?' he asked. I could not, dared not guess. 'I know I look fifty-five, but I'm only thirty-five. It is the life I have to lead, long hours of driving, sometimes twenty-four hours non-stop on these dangerous mountain roads. I keep going on tea and cigarettes!' I admired the dignity and lack of self-pity he displayed. I asked about his family. Just ten days before our arrival his brother, a soldier, had been killed by a terrorist bullet on the Kashmir frontier. He would now, in honour, have to look after his widow and his three children. When she had completed her four-month period of bereavement, during which she cannot leave her house, he would take her into his own home. He had a wife

and two daughters himself and three rooms in his
house. When not driving, he ran a taxi. When he
was away, he rented it out and thus made a small
income. His two daughters must be provided with
dowries, otherwise they wouldn't get husbands,
which is a great disgrace for a Pakistani girl. He
also provided for his ageing parents. It was going
to be much harder for him now that he had his
brother's family to provide for. But he was happy
– he loved his wife and daughters. He never looked
at other women although the opportunity often
presented itself. A fine man, I thought.

We were now on our way up the valley to Swat
by way of the Malakand Pass. The mountains
began to open up around us in huge, spectacular
peaks. It seemed incredible that we could ever get
up to those dizzy heights. We were all tense yet exhilarated at the thought of what lay ahead. Our
first stop was at the ancient temple site of Tahkti-
i-Bhai, a Buddhist monastery dating back to the
fifth century. It was strange to find Buddhism here
in this valley. It was brought here by King Ashoka,
a warrior who was converted from violence to
peace in the third century BC. He liked the piety
and reverence for all life he found in Buddhism.
From here, Buddhism spread to China and Tibet.
We climbed the steep hill to the site and saw the remains of cells, stoupas, temples and courtyards, all
long in ruins. Many Chinese pilgrims used to make
the long journey over the mountains to worship at
this monastery. Many of the lovely Gandharan

artefacts we had seen in the Peshawar museum had been found here. It was easy to imagine the effect on the meditating mind of the awesome landscape. Alas, the White Huns from Asia invaded and destroyed the monastery and the monks fled.

We were soon in Swat, which was teeming with buses, horses and carts, business going on in every corner. Almond blossom was framed by vivid green fields, where small bullocks were ploughing. The steep slopes of the hills had been worked into terraces of green which made a lovely rhythmical pattern, broad and beautiful. Huge schist rocks lay around, many of them holed like Henry Moore sculptures. As we got to the top of the Shangla Pass, the River Swat became so squeezed between high mountains that it had become a fantastic torrent of foaming, whirling, cascading water. On one side of us was the sheer mountainside, while on the other, the valley fell away abruptly in a fantastic cascade of scree.

Here in Swat in the early fourth century BC, Alexander the Great had passed with his army on his way to subdue all India on his march to the ocean, which he believed encircled the earth. He was a great strategist, but he had a hard time subduing the local tribes at Swat, so great and tenacious fighters were they. It was here at Udegram that Alexander crossed the Swat River with part of his army on his way to join up with the rest of the army, which had come through the Khyber Pass. He knew that he would face stiff resistance

beyond Taxila (which we were to visit on our way
back down the KKH). He was delayed at Taxila
for two to three months and then marched his
army onwards in appalling monsoon weather to
the Jehem River. The local Indian Rajah, Porus,
had his army drawn up on one side of the river,
facing Alexander's armies. Porus had three to four
thousand cavalry, three hundred war chariots and
two hundred war elephants. Alexander knew that
his horses would go mad with fright if they had to
face this line of trumpeting, trampling elephants.
Alexander encircled them, let the archers pick off
the mahouts and discharge volleys of spears into
the most vulnerable parts of these elephants. The
maddened beasts stamped many of Alexander's
men underfoot, crushing them, armour and all,
into a bloody pulp. They caught others up in their
trunks and dashed them to the ground and im-
paled still others on their tusks. Then Alexander
forced the elephants and the enemy into a narrower and narrower space and the maddened elephants then started to crush their own men. What
carnage! Porus fought to the bitter end, viewing
the field from the top of his huge war elephant.
Defeated, he faced Alexander. Alexander reined
in his horse and looked at his adversary with admiration. He was a magnificent figure of a man,
over seven feet tall and of great personal beauty.
His bearing had lost none of its pride; his air was
of one brave man meeting another, of a king in
the presence of a king, with whom he had fought

honourably for his kingdom. When Alexander asked him how he wished to be treated, the dignified warrior said, 'Like a king!' Alexander pressed him further. Was there nothing else he wanted for himself? He had only to ask! 'Everything,' Porus told his captor, 'is contained in that one request!'

Alexander's horse, Bucephalos, died in the battle of old age and wounds. Alexander gave him a state funeral and he himself led the procession. He founded a town and called it Bucephala after him. He called another settlement Perita after a favourite dog. These are the things I remember about the great Alexander, not his military campaigns, but I was moved to imagine him and his armies here in Swat, all those centuries ago. (I was riveted to the spot when I saw a completely Greek face here today in Swat.)

We stopped for a short break. I wandered off along the rough road amid those sublime mountains when I heard the voices of children. I followed the voices and came upon a small, shabby building. It was a school, primitive in the extreme. Thirty children squatted on the floor. The teacher stood at the front beside a makeshift blackboard. 'Come in, Madame,' he said in English. He had few resources for teaching these children and his pay was negligible. The children looked curiously at this woman who seemed to be walking about alone in the village. 'Can they say anything in English?' I asked the teacher. He shook his head. 'Let us learn to count to ten in English!' I held up my ten fingers. The children understood at once. 'One, two, three, four … ten,' they called out after me, very pleased with themselves. It was over in ten minutes. When I got back to Ireland, I sent a large parcel of books and pencils to the teacher, but I never knew if he received them.

Not all children were at school, for they could be seen all along the road. They were busy collecting stones which they sell for building houses and they sell water to passing lorry drivers. Every little bit helps the family survive.

'We turn right at Khwazakhala,' said Heider, as if to announce that we would turn right off a busy city street. In fact, we were to turn right up the KKH and over the Shangla Pass to enter a rugged and awesome landscape. We had the great mountain, Nanga Parbat, eighth highest in the world, on our right, now alone and majestic in its gleaming white snow cap, shrouded and mysterious. We were soon stopped by soldiers at a military checkpoint and our papers were examined. These young men, some not much more than boys, seemed in no hurry to let us go. They must hate being posted up here in the snow and the cold. Their little hut was crude and uncomfortable. No alcohol was permitted. We were now in Indus Kohistan, a remote area unwelcoming to outsiders. Here the KKH cuts through the Indus Gorge and the road is so high above the valley that it sent shivers down our spines to see it ahead. Way below us, the Indus, grey with snow melt, tore its way frenetically through a narrow gorge, a foaming fury in a desolation of mountains which rise so high above it that parts of the land see only a few hours of sunshine a day. This road has been called 'the most dramatic of all Pakistan's mountains'. We could not imagine a more dramatic one.

We reached Swat in time for dinner. I had always loved the title 'the Wali of Swat' and was hoping to meet the august gentleman. Our hotel had obviously not been occupied for some time, for the sheets were damp and the electricity unreliable. Not for the first time, I laid my raincoat on the bed and slept on it. The Wali's house lay behind the hotel, but he no longer lived in it. Once one of many small independent states, Swat was taken over by the Pakistani government in 1969 and the Wali and his family left the valley for the town. The house, green, long and low in a colonial style, is surprisingly modest. The garden was overgrown. I peered through the shutters and saw that the rooms were still furnished, rooms for when the Wali received his guests. It has not yet been decided what to do with this historic house.

The handcraft shop in the hotel had many beautiful things on offer – ruby and emerald necklaces, embroidered cloths, cashmere scarves. I couldn't resist a beautiful old patchwork quilt in dark colours with concentric circles, triangles and parallels weaving in and out of each other into a harmonious whole. It is a real work of art. An American woman was examining these quilts with an expert eye. 'I've come here especially to buy these. You won't find the like of such hangings much longer. They take months to make. Most of these are at least twenty years old.' My own piece hangs on the wall of the room in which I now write. Late in the evening, when walking about, I came upon a small handcraft shop at the back of the hotel. An old man kept some pieces for sale, but he told me that he got few sales because the tourists who came patronised the hotel shop. In bed that night, I decided to get up early to give him some custom. His shop was open at 6.30 a.m. and I made a purchase of a beautiful cashmere shawl.

The next day we had an eleven-hour journey to Chilas ahead of us. The road became so narrow, the mountains so precipitous, the fall to the valley below so immense that every time a vehicle passed our vans, we closed our eyes and held our breath. We saw our first fresh landslides and rock falls on the road and several lorry accidents. Decidedly, the going was getting rough. We stopped for a drivers' tea break. These drivers did these arduous journeys on nothing more than tea and cigarettes every two hours. In every slit in these mountains, small-time family entrepreneurs had set up primitive cafés to supply the drivers. We were always the only women to patronise them. No women were visible and we were warned not to try to take photos of women we might see in these courtyards from our high vantage points. I don't know what the locals made of us, but it couldn't have been flattering. At that tea stop, we watched a century-old scene – two groups of men sitting in two circles resolving a dispute over the ownership of trees.

At Chilas, the Pakistani and Chinese teams met up after hacking and dynamiting their way through to each other. From then on, the design of the bridges was Chinese. The loss of over four hundred men in the construction of the highway is marked here by a memorial stone. A separate Chinese cemetery stands, forlorn and sad, nearby. I cannot imagine that the relatives are ever able to visit these graves.

The next day, we were off at 7 a.m. for a twelve-hour drive to Skardu along the Indus Valley Road. This was a detour off the main road to Gilgit, undertaken for the breathtaking scenery we would witness. The Indus here divides the Himalayas from the Karakorams. The road soon became just a notch in the sheer granite face of the mountain. Above us towered huge snow-covered peaks and below us, the non-stop fury of the Indus. It was hard to believe that we could come through all this alive. There were many blind corners.

No one spoke. We arrived in our hotel late in the evening, a new hotel on Kachura Lake – the Shangri-la of Pakistan, thus called for its exquisite position, hidden away in the high mountains. The water was a deep turquoise blue, herons lined the edge, high on their stilts, and white swans glided over the surface. The moon and stars shone brilliantly that night and the water gave back the light almost as brilliantly. The hotel was composed of low pavilions in Chinese style. We remembered that the people here had originally come from Tibet and Ladakh.

The next day was devoted entirely to a visit to the remote Shigar Lake that marks the entrance to the Karakoram Range. The lake is so isolated that it can only be reached by a jeep track. The people in Shigar Valley live very quietly and are said to dislike outsiders. Few tourists ever trouble their peace. The lake itself was so isolated that we felt we must have been the first people to look upon it. The silence was almost frightening. The Mir's house is now abandoned. When the government took over the valley, he gave his house freely to his people. We wandered into the courtyard where women were washing clothes and gossiping. We saw the large open-air platforms surrounded by water where the Mir stood and viewed his people. The remains of a large garden now boasted clumps of wild daffodils.

The next day, we returned along the dangerous Indus Valley road to Gilgit. The side valleys were blocked with snow and we could hear the creaking of moving snow. We reached Gilgit in the afternoon. After the smaller villages we had passed through, it seemed like a metropolis. It's a busy town and has an airport, but it is as much a tribal town as any of the others on the highway.

What we especially remember of Gilgit is the exciting polo match we watched, so different from the orderly, civilised polo matches at home. Here, the players ride bareback and whack the ball furiously. The horses gallop and brake and somehow don't kill each other or the riders. A band of local men play lively tunes and after every goal there is wild cheering from the crowd of spectators. People danced and sang. Nobody paid any attention to us, the only women there.

In the evening, the weather turned dark and ominous. It rained all night, the first rain that had fallen since we'd arrived in the country. We knew that rain was dangerous – it made the scree and mud unstable. In the morning, rain was still falling and news came that rock and mud slides had closed the road from Gulmit, above Hunza, to the Chinese border. Qumar was worried. He telephoned and faxed and finally was advised not to try for the Kunjerab Pass and the border. We would instead spend a second night in Gilgit and visit the Hunza Valley from there. We set out at 11 a.m. for Hunza under gloomy skies. The mountains closed in on us, huge, grey-brown, dead and menacing. The drivers kept a constant watch for slides and rock falls. They twice had to stop the vans and use shovels to clear the way.

Then we came into the Hunza Valley itself. It was amazing to come upon such a fertile valley. It was the most remote and beautiful of all the valleys we had seen. The Hunza River is the only one that cuts across the spine of the Karakorams, creating dangerous rapids as it goes. Clever irrigation has allowed a network of channels to bring water from the river to irrigate the valley. Even wheat and maize can be grown here. People used to live by robbery and slave trading. Now, it's peaceful and profitable.

The people are Ismailis, a branch of Islam which came from Iran via Afghanistan three hundred years ago. It is an unusual branch of Islam, for in its formularies there is no concept of set prayers – prayer is a personal matter – and there is no prostration before Allah, no mosques either, just a community hall. They view the Aga Khan as their God and he looks after them, providing money for clinics and schools. The children here are better dressed than in the other valleys and many wear smart school uniforms. The famed longevity of the people of Hunza is said to be due to their diet – apricot oil is claimed to prevent cancer. On hearing this news, we all rush into a small shop which sells this oil and overwhelm the little old owner with orders. I eventually get mine in a tomato ketchup bottle! Since the opening of the KKH, the diet of the Hunza people has changed. They no longer eat so many apricots and so much buckwheat and they don't live as long.

Rising up above the river and the valley are mighty brown scree slopes, giving way to the immense snowy peaks of the Ragaposhie mountain range. We stopped at Chalt near Hunza and had the most exciting geological experience it's possible to have. Fifty million years ago, the Indian geological plate ploughed into the Asian plate, causing a stupendous collision which violently pushed up the land into what we call the Himalayas, the Karakorams and the Hindu Kush. The highway here in Hunza runs along the edge of the Asian plate and we could see, distinctly exposed to our eyes, the two plates, with a multitude of different rocks and minerals thrown up from the depths of the earth and pushed against each other. This rise in the land is still continuing today at a rate of five centimetres a year. Nanga Parbat is rising faster than the rest, at eight centimetres a year. These unstable conditions make the whole north of Pakistan a volatile earthquake zone. Many thousands were killed in Kohistan Indus in 1974.

The Mir of Hunza, like the Wali of Swat, is a name which trips exotically off the tongue. He is no longer in residence. It is another one of those little tribal valleys, so long self-governing, which were taken over by the Pakistani government in the 1970s and 1980s. The Mir moved out of his royal palace in 1974 and gave it to his people. It had been the royal palace of Hunza for 750 years. It was very impressive, sitting high on a ridge in a superb landscape. The house and fort fell into ruin but were reassembled by British and Pakistani architects and are now very handsome.

❧

Although we had managed to see Hunza on a dry day, it began to rain heavily again on our return journey along the perilous road to Gilgit. The sky grew black and menacing so that the grim walls of the mountains seemed to shut out the sky above us, while huge overhanging rocks with gaping cracks threatened to split apart at any moment and crash down upon us. Shale and melted ice poured over the road, which was visibly crumbling before our eyes. The squeaking sound of moving glaciers alarmed us mightily. Qumar stopped the van and told us not to worry – both drivers were very experienced and could sense possible danger very quickly. He put me in the front of the second van with orders to look out for likely rock falls. We were not to shout, as shouting could start a rock fall! That journey was more hellish than any journey I had ever done. Everyone was tense. The gloom and darkness made my search of the road ahead all the more difficult. My eyes were sore, my head tense. The drivers somehow negotiated their way around several fresh rock falls. Everyone knew that at any moment, a great rock could loosen and fall down upon our vans. It was with the greatest relief that we finally drew up at our hotel in Gilgit.

The next morning, the skies were clear and there was no rain. Could we have got to the Chinese border after all? Qumar was adamant that the road would still be closed. There was no question now of following the original plan of flying from Gilgit to Islamabad, a flight down between the mountains which is known to be extremely dramatic. Conditions were too bad. We must leave early and return back down the Karakoram to Becham, completing the journey in the day, at least a twelve-hour drive. We had a picnic lunch in a tiny café in a slit in the rocks in Kohistan. I watched as a bearded young man entered a small patch of green beside the river. He took off his gun and gun belt, laid them on the grass and proceeded to wash his face, forearms and feet in the river. He then turned, faced Mecca, prostrated himself several times, rose, put on his gun and went on his way. Indus Kohistan is particularly known for its lawlessness and hatred of strangers. Every man here carries a gun, not only for protection, but for hunting in the valleys.

I took a short walk in this wonderful mountain air and came upon an old woman with her back carefully turned away from me, retching and vomiting at the side of the road. I held out a Paracetamol tablet to her, touching her lightly on the arm. With alacrity, she struck my arm away. I, a foreign woman, disgusted her.

All the way back to Becham, we come upon scree and rock falls. Lorry drivers are at work with shovels trying to clean the road. We came upon a huge rock which had fallen right in the middle of the road. 'It is not more than an hour old,' said Heider. It could well have fallen on us and crushed us. We were not yet out of danger. The Pakistani army, which is responsible for keeping the road clear, is on holiday. It is the big religious feast of Eid on the morrow and everyone is on holiday. What does a rock or two matter? What were the drivers to do? No vehicle could pass this rock, for it blocked the narrow road completely. On each side of it, several vehicles are waiting to pass. A truck driver ties a rope to one end of the boulder and attaches it to his lorry. The lorry pulls on the rope, with little success. The drivers all put their shoulders to the boulder and rock it to and fro until, inch by desperate inch, it gives way. There is just room for one vehicle to pass on the outside valley side. We pass in our turn with what seems like three inches between ourselves and perdition in the valley below. Qumar says he can hear an avalanche beginning. Again, nobody speaks.

Our next tea stop was at a small café in a valley opening on the banks of a fast-flowing river. There is the usual primitive arrangement: the whole family is baking, stewing, making tea, taking orders. As I sip my tea outside the café, I notice an old man, very tall and regal with pale blue eyes and a white beard, quite unlike the other men. He is sitting on a very dirty chair inside the café. He gesticulates to Qumar to come to him. Qumar talks with him, then turns towards me. 'This old man would like to shake you by the hand. Please come!'

I advance towards him and he gets up from his chair and insists that I sit down in it myself. I can smell the dirt. 'I was the Wali of Swat's butler, you know. I looked after everything, hired staff, gardeners, kitchen men. He trusted me completely. I welcomed his guests and looked after them. Now he has left Swat, I have come back here but I have nothing to do. You are very, very welcome, Madame. My house is your house. You can stay in my house tonight and sleep in whatever room you choose. There is my house.' He brings me to the window and points into the distance. There is an immediate hubbub among the men and they scowl menacingly. 'What has happened?' I ask Qumar.

'They do not like him talking to a stranger and showing his house. These people do not like foreigners!' I hastily shake the old man by the hand and retreat as quickly and as gracefully as I can. He must have learned these courtesies when working for the Wali of Swat.

When we arrived at Becham late that evening, we were very tired but we had made it – we were through, unharmed, and had in our heads images of beauty we would never forget.

After the many excitements of the day and twelve cramped hours in a minibus, we were glad to reach Becham, a small but important junction which we had passed through on our upward journey from Peshawar to Swat. It was to be our last stop on the highway. Tomorrow we would hit the Grand Trunk Road which runs from Calcutta to Kabul. It would take us to Rawalpindi, our final stop in this amazing journey. The hotel was very basic, more like a military barracks than a hotel, but we didn't mind. Having been on the roof of the world, comforts or lack of them were somehow unimportant. My room was sparse and bleak, but the great roar from the Indus outside my window more than made up for that. What a sound to sleep by!

As we were claiming our keys and our bags in the lobby, Qumar beckoned to me. Could I join him and the driver in his room for a drink before dinner? Although strictly illegal to drink alcohol in Pakistan, he had somehow procured some grappa. I supposed we were to celebrate having made it. Washed and restored, I made my way to Qumar's room at the appointed hour. Qumar is there, and despite his lined face, he looks magnificent, even regal in his fresh white tunic and black shawl. He is sharing the room with Heider, an unusual and generous gesture on Qumar's part, for the driver is expected to sleep in his bus. Our grappa is poured, our glasses raised and they tell me that I am their 'sister', that they love me, that I appreciate all they do, that I love their country and its ways. I reply in kind and mean it. Qumar tells me he has a special reason for inviting me on this occasion. It is not, after all, a celebration of having 'made' the highway. It is a personal matter. He had maintained an admirable reserve all throughout our trip, a reserve combined with a spontaneous charm which was much admired by all of us. Now I was going to hear something of his personal life.

'You may have noticed how often I have been telephoning Islamabad these past weeks. I was phoning my wife and for a very special reason. She may be going to have a baby and she is counting her days. I am so happy. We have been married for six months now. I love her very much. She has given up everything for me and I am ready to do the same for her. I shall look after her always. She is not Pakistani, she is Japanese. She is a tour guide like myself. We first met in this very hotel where we are staying tonight. It is a kind of anniversary we are celebrating.'

He went on slowly. 'I am so glad you can join my celebration. But I must tell you that I have been married before.' His handsome face tightened as he looked back in his mind's eye at that wife and that event. She, too, was Japanese and a tour guide. 'Japanese parties come here from time to time to do the highway and bring their tour leader with them. I long ago knew that I could not marry a Pakistani woman as was, of course, expected of me by all my family. They have little or no education, their thoughts are on their faces and their bodies, as youth and a dowry are their only appeal to a husband. Here in Pakistan, there is no conception of companionship, of mutual understanding in marriage. Yes, I know it's men who have dictated the roles. I do not like it but it is so. My first wife was chic, sophisticated, cultivated. Here was a woman I could share my thoughts with, here was a woman I could worship and care for. My whole soul opened to her. My father, a senator in parliament, and my mother at first objected, but when they saw my happiness, they accepted my choice.' I could see his face looking back to those days and smiling a secret smile. How romantic, I thought. I listened quietly and attentively.

'My wife, older than I, was very anxious to have a baby. Within months, she told me that she was expecting our child. I surrounded her with every tenderness and my mother, too, could not have been more kind. My wife seemed anxious about her pregnancy. She felt she could not trust the Pakistani doctors to look after her. She would trust herself only to a good Japanese doctor whom she knew. No, she had no faith in Pakistani doctors. She had not seen her parents since before her marriage [they had not been able to make the long journey from Japan for the ceremony]. What would I think of her plan to take a short holiday in Japan and have herself checked up by a doctor there? You can imagine how sad I was to hear this. I assured her that we would get an excellent doctor, English trained, to look after her. She was charmingly adamant. I had to let her go, but on the promise that she would return to me in a month's time. I tried to prepare for this long interval by telling myself that life would be even richer when she returned and our child would be born. She telephoned regularly. Everything was going well, it seemed, but her gynaecologist had advised her to stay in Japan for the birth, for he feared certain complications. She knew I would understand. She knew I loved her enough for that. Then at last came the news to the overwrought husband: a baby had been born, safe and well, a boy. It would not be long until her return. My parents were over-joyed both for me and for themselves. A month passed. We waited for her to come. Another month passed and still she did not return. There was always an excuse for the delay.

'Finally a whole year passed. I grew ill and de-pressed. My mother mourned inwardly to see how her beloved son had lost his health. He had re-mained faithful in body and soul all this time to his wife. It was hard. After a second year had passed my father came to me and said, "You must divorce her! You deserve a life other than this perpetual misery!" I delayed, hesitated, reluctant to give up hope. Finally I agreed. I divorced her, Muslim style. Another year and a half passed and my bachelor days were as miserable as ever. I could not help thinking of that son of mine in Japan whom I had never seen. He had a Japanese name. Then, six months ago, as I have told you, in this very hotel I met my second wife. She, too, is Japanese and a tour leader. She, too, is chic, cultivated, travelled. We fell deeply in love. She told me she wanted to marry me. I would give my soul for her. This evening, on the telephone, she told me that she be-lieved she was pregnant, that she was counting her days. You can imagine my joy. In two days we will be in Islamabad and I want you to meet her and all your friends too for I have come to love you all.' He stretched out his hands as if to embrace us. He knew we would like her, for we were educated, as she was.

'Please,' I said, 'let both of you be our guests at dinner. That will make us very happy.' I was to wait for the end of the story for another two days. When it came, it was to be a shock to me.

We left Becham very early the next morning. The air of relaxation in the bus was palpable. We had come through. We had made it. It would be a long time before the exhilaration of these majestic mountains faded from our minds. We were descending from the highway to the hill station country where the British took refreshment from the heat of the plain.

The countryside was lush, the air dry and fresh. As we drove through the Manseghra Valley where our driver grew up and where his parents still lived, he became so emotional that he had to stop the bus to do pee-pee! No dangers on the highway had ever had this effect on him. A short stop at Abbotsbad followed. It was our first glimpse of a British military station, the station where John Abbot had been High Commissioner, distributing justice to the Indian people. The station must have made the colonists feel a little at home, with its English-style houses and its gardens. I walked into an English church, St Luke's, where I saw a prayer book in Urdu. There are twenty-five Anglican families in the congregation. Even more surprising was a Presbyterian church, a Roman Catholic church and even a Brethren hall.

Decidedly, the British brought their religion with them to this exotic country. Heider told us that he himself had been a soldier in the army in the 19th Frontier Force for nine years. These years had given him the discipline and the stamina to be a mountain driver on the Karakoram Highway. He pointed out some beautiful horses which were being trained here for the Pakistani cavalry, for duty on the Kashmir frontier. We knew how tensions ran high there. In the distance, we could see the high, dreamy peaks of the Kashmiri hills, the disputed territory.

In the early afternoon, we reached the Grand Trunk Road, an unimaginable pulsating throng of vehicles of every kind – lorries, bicycles, rickshaws, bullock carts and put-puts, with their big spots and coloured sides like ladybirds with folded wings. Heider drove furiously through this throng so that for the first time I was alarmed. He reassured me that he knew the road well and we were quite safe. We had an hour's stop at Taxila, the meeting point of big trade routes from Afghanistan and many cultures. Alexander the Great had stayed here, discussing politics and philosophy.

Preparations were going on feverishly for the forthcoming Feast of Eid, the reminder of the sacrifice demanded of Abraham. It is a great feast in the Muslim calendar. There were sheep markets everywhere, where animals were being picked out for sacrifice. Superbly groomed sheep with henna and ribbons little knew what fate awaited them. Animals, said Qumar, had to be perfect for sacrifice – straight horns, not less than eighteen months old with two teeth. Henna and brushes are on sale everywhere and fruit, too, in abundance. Qumar tells us that he will celebrate the feast himself – he will have just such an animal sacrificed at his home. The butcher will ritually kill it and, after nine o'clock prayers, he will give away most of the meat to relatives or to those too poor to buy their own sheep. Everyone will celebrate. No one will work. Even the soldiers who control the Karakoram Highway will not work. Everyone will be on the streets. He promises us to do what he can to let us see something of the celebrations on the morrow. He is very excited. We spend the night in Rawalpindi in great comfort.

The next day, the feast itself, we drove to Islamabad. It is a 'made' capital, its streets laid out symmetrically in long lines with trees and flowerbeds, all very different from the happy, chaotic towns we have seen. The Faisal Mosque is magnificent, a great Muslim cathedral in dazzling white. It is the colour of a desert tent, its decorations the pale blue of the desert sky and the sand colour of the desert, the desert where Arabs had their beginnings. Four tall minarets send the call of Muslims up to heaven. Qumar tries to get permission for us to enter the mosque for nine o'clock prayers, but it's no use: women are not allowed in. We peer through the glass doors instead.

In the evening, we are to meet Quamar's wife at dinner. I'm very curious. My phone rings. They are in the lobby, waiting for me. I hurry down and see her, slim and elegant beside him. She is very cold and self-possessed. Her eyes are cold and unsmiling. I'm sure she doesn't want to be here, doesn't want to meet us. Qumar excuses himself: he has instructions for the driver. Would I look after his wife for a few minutes? I beckon her to a seat and sit down beside her. To open the conversation, I ask her how she likes Pakistan. She looks away. 'I do not like it at all. It is no place for an educated woman. Paris or London are my natural home. I like concerts, the theatre. There is none of that here. The women here have not two ideas in their heads. They are simply sex objects or mothers. I cannot even go the market without being stared at.'

'Qumar has told me the good news of your baby,' I say. 'What with that and your charming husband, you'll surely be happy here.'

She looks away once more. 'I shall have to go back to Japan to have the baby. I do not trust Pakistani doctors. I have not told Qumar yet, but he will understand. He is sure of me.'

In a flash, I saw the pattern repeating itself. These two Japanese women, no longer in their first youth, wanted a handsome non-Japanese father for their child, but as a husband, he wasn't included. I wept inwardly for his innocent, romantic soul and for the hurt that was surely in store for him. Some years later, I was to learn, indirectly, that this is indeed what happened.

The next day, we left Pakistan. When we reached the airport, I made a speech of thanks to Qumar and Heider and Majeed, thanks that were well won and gratefully given. I was the last to leave the bus. Heider approached me. 'I love you. I want to give you something – big stone,' he said, and he put into my hand what I took to be a large, heavy stone ring. 'Very old. I pick it up in Takht-i-Bahi.' I thought it rather large and ugly, but I thanked him for it and we said goodbye. During the flight back to London, I looked again at this rough object and, turning it round, I discovered carving on the front of it – a woman's head. What could it be? I knew Takht-i-Bahi was a centre of Gandharan art, and as I had bought a book on the subject in the place itself, I opened it and there I saw the very same head of a woman cited as a traditional design. I was overcome. Had Heider picked up this ancient ring there and given it to me? What should I do with it? I knew it was illegal to take any ancient objects out of the country, but who would know if I did? I would think about that when I got home …

I did think about it. My conscience got the better of me and I determined to give it back. Some time later, I was in Oxford and had the opportunity to consult an expert at the Ashmolean Museum. I asked him how to go about returning the ring to Pakistan. He took it from me and scrutinised it closely. 'I'm afraid this is a fake. I'm surprised that they're still making them.' I was shocked, more for what had been 'passed off' on me than for the object itself. Did Heider know? Had he acted in good faith or in bad, I wondered. I preferred to think that he didn't know.

# Lebanon and Syria

## *1999*

We wanted to see Lebanon, recently emerged from a civil war such as we were experiencing in Northern Ireland. It was the home of the famous poet, Khalil Gibron. Syria was a mysterious, enigmatic country seldom visited by tourists, but there was Damascus to be seen and Aleppo and the famous River Euphrates.

We had heard as much about Beirut as the world has heard about Belfast. We felt that we would recognise what we would see – bullet holes in the walls, vacant spaces where buildings had once been, a peace line to keep different cultures from killing each another, a multitude of journalists analysing the 'situation', PhD students writing theses on the political situation. In Belfast, there were two main factions at war with each other, but in Lebanon, there were at least three – Maronite Christians, Muslims and Druze (an extreme Muslim sect). Like our own, their situation had been created by the past.

Geographical Syria has been a perennial jigsaw puzzle, constantly taken apart and reassembled. Both Lebanon and Syria were under Turkish rule for four hundred years, but in 1916 there was an

Arab revolt against the Turks, a revolt in which T.E. Laurence distinguished himself. Only in 1945 did Syria and Lebanon become independent. All was well until 1948, when a new menace appeared – the state of Israel was created. Vast numbers of Palestinian refugees flooded into Lebanon, and in 1975, a war broke out between Syria and Israel, who were the main players in the game. Massacres and revolts followed each other inexorably. Fighting continued until 1989 and the peace line was only dismantled in 1991. (Our Belfast peace line is still in place.) From 1985, hostage-taking became an instrument of war and was practised by all sides. We all knew about the Irishman Brian Keenan's time as a hostage in Beirut because he has written his story. Now, in 1999, peace had descended upon this troubled nation and it was possible for courageous people to visit it freely. We knew that tourists would be welcome in these circumstances.

In Beirut, we did see the bullet holes and the empty spaces and the run-down condition of the city, but we also saw the crowds of liberated people strolling along the beautiful seafront in the warm evening air and crowding into the multitude of busy little restaurants which dotted the promenade. They were eating, drinking and laughing – life had reasserted itself. This beautiful city, with its Mediterranean coastline, once a Garden City of the Ottoman Turks, had, under the French mandate, become chic and sophisticated. But as we know, civilisation is only skin deep. This city had descended into savagery. Now it had a chance to reinvent itself. We were there just at the right time.

'Where are you from?' came the well-known question as were walking about the fine archaeological museum.

'From Northern Ireland,' we chanted back. A tall Arab grabbed me by both hands and held them up high in his own.

'Hooray! Hooray! IRA-Hezbollah, IRA-Hezbollah!' We received the accolade as discreetly as we could.

We looked at famous places in the south of the country – Tyre and Sidon, which Alexander the Great took and where Jesus passed, the stupendous temple of Jupiter in Baalbek, then north to the city of Byblos, which gave us the Greek name *biblia*, books and the Bible. This was a special place for us literary students. From Egypt, Byblos imported papyrus, made it into scrolls, then re-exported it. In return, Egypt bought fragrant cedar wood from Lebanon. Solomon built his palace of this wood. So famous were the cedars of Lebanon that we made a special excursion to see them. We were disappointed. Instead of a forest of handsome trees, we saw only the few that remained and the whole site was tourist-worn.

Our Lebanese guide, a young university graduate in English, was sophisticated and bored. A group of middle-aged men and women from Ireland didn't inspire him. When we got to the lovely little port of Byblos, with its charming fishing harbour and the remains of a once-great city perched upon it, he told us to explore the ruins on our own, he was going for a coffee! Many of the group decided to do the same thing, doubtless expecting him to show us the ruins afterwards. I decided to sally forth on my own so as to have more time for exploration. I walked confidently at first. I made my way through rough grasses and small flowering shrubs pushing their way through fragments of statuary, capitals and bases of pillars fallen over the centuries by the hand of time or man. There were no signposts. Where were the Sacred Lakes, the Temple of Baal, the Roman theatre? I soon got lost. I tried this path and that and couldn't find the sites. It was ridiculous to think that I couldn't find my way in a circumscribed place like this. I must get hold of myself and search methodically. I was still going around in circles and getting more and more anxious. Where were the others? Why was there not a single tourist about? The emptiness and the silence were unnerving. I was alone in a silent wilderness. There was nothing to be seen or heard but the sighing of the wind over the long grasses amid the toppled stones. It had a strange, out-of-time, dreamlike quality which held me in a strange spell. I felt that I could be there forever.

It was a huge relief to come suddenly on a gap in a wall and a way out into the town. A Maronite priest stood before me and, seeing my puzzled expression, asked in French if he could help me. He was poised and sophisticated. No doubt these Maronites, as I had been told, looked down on the Muslims in their midst. I learned from him that Maronites take their name from St Maro, a hermit of Syria who died in the fifth century. They differ from the Orthodox in their interpretation of that mysterious essence, the Nature of Christ. They are in communion with Rome but can marry. Nevertheless, the Maronites here have their own political agenda. In 1980, under Israeli cover, they massacred thousands of Palestinian refugees in the camps of Chatila and Sabra, massacres that have haunted the conscience of men ever since. Religion was once again invoked to kill and maim.

We climbed out of Byblos away from the coast up into the mountains and the beautiful Qadisha Valley, spotted here and there with monasteries, until we came to Bcharre, a stone-built village falling away in flowery terraces into a river gorge. We had come here to pay our respects to a Lebanese poet, Khalil Gibran (1883–1931). He was born here and is buried here. He is widely read and loved the world over. A deeply spiritual man, he rebelled against civil and religious authority. His first work, *Spirits Rebellious*, was condemned and burned by the Maronite Church and he was excommunicated. He and his family had to emigrate to the United States, where he continued to write and paint. He wrote copiously about love and longing, desire, despair and the meaning of life. His poem 'The Prophet' is a kind of bible for some people.

We looked through the house-museum hidden away in the trees, then sat out on the narrow terrace and thought of him. Someone quoted his verse by heart. We lingered in that wooded garden hemmed in by trees and flowers until it was time to go. And go we did, for there was a new adventure ahead of us – we were to cross the border and go into Syria, that unknown, intriguing country, a police state, a tourist-free land.

The great names – Damascus, Aleppo, Palmyra – were to be seen. Excitement grew. What would our reception be like? Would we be searched? We were to change both bus and guide at the border. We drew up at a small hut. A thin, swarthy man got on. He was to be our Syrian guide. He seemed nervous and hesitant when speaking and even stuttered from time to time. The Lebanese guide and driver exchanged knowing smiles. I didn't like the complacent superiority that these smiles betrayed. I could see that the Lebanese fancied themselves as superior to these uncouth Syrians. We said goodbye to our Lebanese guide without regret.

During the ten days we were to spend in Syria, our Syrian guide, Ahmet, may have been unsophisticated, but was knowledgeable, helpful, kind, enthusiastic and anxious to show us his country. He responded at once to our curiosity and soon lost his nervousness. He invited us all to his home, a small, clean, sparse but comfortable apartment, and introduced us to his wife and children, gave us tea, invited questions. His wife was closely covered. Did she mind? No, she did not. She would feel naked without her headscarf. She was dedicated to the education of her two small children. They would learn languages, maybe become guides like her husband.

'Yes,' said Ahmet, 'Syria *is* a police state. I have just had a phone call from the security police about this group. They are tracking us.' He smiled. 'I told them that there was nothing to fear.' We smiled too.

We had much to learn about this closed society and its rich heritage. Like all Middle Eastern countries, it has been crossed by successive invaders who have come at it from all directions. Empires, religions and trade had come and gone over the centuries and left layer upon layer of civilisation behind them. The notion of one country leaving its home and setting out to 'free' another country is far older than the present-day 'crusade' by Britain and the US to 'free' Iraq. The Crusaders had the same agenda – they wanted to take Jerusalem from the Infidel. They left England and France to make their way to Palestine and Damascus was repeatedly attacked by the crusading Franks in the process. There followed four hundred years of rule by the Turkish Empire before Syria became an independent republic.

General Assad, president, is in fact a dictator. Ahmet was surprisingly frank about how Assad came to power. In 1970, he ousted the civilian government and declared himself president and has held supreme power ever since. In 1973, there was a huge revolt against him by a Sunni Muslim sect centred around the town of Hama, which we were now visiting. This deeply conservative sect wanted Assad to make Islam a state religion, and when he refused to do so (he himself was an Alawi Muslim), the Muslim Brotherhood revolted and took up arms against him. Assad showed his ruthlessness in the face of this. He brutally crushed the revolt at a cost of many thousands of lives. As we passed through Hama, Ahmet pointed to a large high-rise hotel. 'He had that hotel erected exactly over the trench where the rebels are buried.' We shuddered at the thought of being guests there.

We were surprised that Ahmet spoke so openly. He pointed to the women walking in the street in Hama. 'You can see how conservative a city this still is. The women are heavily veiled, more so than in any other part of Syria.' Yet, if you looked closely, you could sometimes see, underneath the chadors, painted nails, lipstick, smart shoes, fancy stockings. We were electrified to see one young woman in a short skirt and high heels with a black plastic bag over her face, slits cut out for the eyes. It gave new meaning to the word 'tokenism'.

We lingered by the river, the ancient Orontes, which has dug itself a deep bed in the flat, monotonous plain. A system of irrigation has harnessed the water here. The Norias of Hama are famous, giant wooden water wheels which turn at various speeds and throw up the river water from their blades into canals which are carried upon great arches, bringing water to gardens and fountains in this otherwise scorched town. We watched as small boys swung on the blades of the Norias and rode the wheels down into the river and up again, dripping, laughing, triumphant. Such fun was, of course, denied to little girls. We sat on the terrace of the café overlooking the river and watched the giant wheels turn as countless other people had done before us.

We followed the Orontes Valley until we came to an ancient city with a lovely name, Apamea. It was very hot and we were the only visitors in that empty space. The site stands on a promontory above the river and all around it stretched endless lush grasslands. Apamea was once a Greek city, then a Roman military headquarters where instruments of war were housed – not tanks or guns, but war elephants, six hundred of them, a stud of 30,000 mares and 300 stallions whose home was the grasslands. I shut my eyes and tried to imagine the amazing vitality of this city, the limitless grasslands, the neighing of horses, the trumpeting of elephants, the march of soldiers.

The loveliness of Apamea, now in ruins, lay in its long colonnaded avenues of graceful pillars. The pillars, long fallen, had been re-erected by archaeologists to mark the main roads of the city. We dodged from the shade of one pillar to another to escape the scorching sun. Everywhere, we could see the vestiges of a once thriving city, paving stones on roads rutted by chariot wheels, doorways leading nowhere, roofless temples and empty civic buildings. Mark Antony made his plans here for a military campaign against the Armenians. Cleopatra came from Egypt to be with him. She accompanied him as far as the Euphrates before turning back again via Apamea to Egypt, there to await his return. Now all was hot, still and silent. Only the occasional noise of a young man on a motorbike offering to take us from one part of the site to another disturbed the silence of the great ruined city. This experience again overcame us and made us all strangely silent.

Damascus, that magic name, was before us. Our hotel was relatively modern, impersonal, sitting outside the old city wall. We would spend our time inside these walls in a city said to be one of the oldest inhabited cities in the world. Belfast, by comparison, is a newborn child. The Umayyad mosque was to be our first destination, our first prize in old Damascus. It's extremely holy for all Muslims, being the fourth holiest place in Islam after Mecca, Medina and the Dome of the Rock in Jerusalem. Pilgrims were pouring into the mosque as we arrived. They come from all over the world and even infidels like ourselves are allowed to visit it.

Who were the Umayyads? They were an Arab dynasty who ruled a huge empire in the seventh century, an empire which stretched from India to Spain and whose capital was the city of Damascus. This dynasty is hated by many strict Muslims because it was artistic, relaxed and tolerant. The Umayyads wished to build a mosque in Damascus that would be the glory of Islam. It still is. We knew that we were to visit something very special.

Before we could enter the precincts, we had to pass through the visitors' entrance to be properly prepared. The unsmiling woman attendant, who obviously didn't approve of us, thrust a bundle of black chadors at us and with her hands indicated that we must cover up completely from head to foot. We looked at one another in this alien guise and wanted to laugh but dared not. We felt like actors on a stage where we didn't know our lines. We then passed into the open courtyard of the mosque and stood gazing at what we saw. It was exquisitely beautiful with that space, serenity and mathematical harmony you find everywhere in Muslim architecture and design. It was pure poetry to the eye and to the mind.

What we were looking at was in fact three thousand years of history in stone. It had had many incarnations. The site was first a pagan temple, then the Romans came to Syria and, as their chief god was Jupiter, they built a newer and bigger temple on the site and dedicated it to him. Then the drama of Christianity came to Damascus. In the sixth century, under the Emperor Constantine, the East Rome Empire was ordered to become Christian and all pagan worship was forbidden. The temple of Jupiter was transformed into a Christian church and dedicated to John the Baptist. Next came the Arabs, who, having captured Damascus in 636, wished to build a temple to their gods. They took over the Church of St John the Baptist in 708 and built a great mosque in its place, which was what we were now beholding. Thousands of expert craftsmen were brought in from Constantinople and elsewhere to beautify it. The Prayer Hall was hung with 606 lanterns of gold, the arcaded walls of the courtyard were adorned with exquisite mosaics and the ground was paved with marble. The proportions all harmonise, the classical arcades which run around the courtyard and the mosaics which remain of the originals are green and gold, depicting lively natural scenes, unusual in Islam, landscapes of greenery and water, a stream, a kiosk, villas, palaces. It's no wonder that the people of the desert pictured paradise as a garden. The Koran says, 'This is the Paradise which the righteous have been promised. It is watered by running streams, eternal are its fruits, eternal are is shades.'

In the courtyard, people spoke in whispers. Groups of women in black chadors flitted across the vast space like flocks of blackbirds. We were told they were Iranian women who came with their husbands but who were forbidden to pray with them. I looked into the face of one of these women – she was extremely beautiful under her black garments and was holding two children by the hand. I could see that all three were excited to be here in this holy place. The children were pulling their mother by the hand towards the Prayer Hall, where their father had preceded them. At an ablution fountain in the courtyard, half a dozen men were silently and carefully washing their feet and forearms in preparation for worship. We took off our shoes and moved quietly into the Prayer Hall and remained at the back where, as women, we were permitted to be.

It was impossible not to be impressed by the sight of hundreds of men prostrating themselves in unison in the direction of Mecca. There was no hierarchy, no seats, no furniture, no vestments, little ritual, nothing but rich carpets to prevent the head from touching the bare floor. There was only the niche, the mihrab, to indicate the direction of Mecca and the minbar, the pulpit for the imam, the teacher, to address the faithful on Fridays and on special occasions. He stands on the second step of the minbar, the first being reserved for the Prophet, the Supreme Teacher.

Muslims differ from Christians in one important way – their worship does not involve any enactment of a mystery, as does Christianity in the Eucharist. The Muslim simply faces Mecca, birthplace of Mohammed, and prays for obedience to the will of Allah as set out in the Koran. Islam, however, reveres Jesus, views Him as a great prophet sent by Allah and believes He is born of the Virgin Mary and the Holy Spirit. Jesus, they say, did not really die on the Cross; instead, a substitute was put in his place and Jesus was taken directly up to God, where He lives outside time and space. One day, He will descend again from Heaven and will come by the Minaret of Jesus, which is part of this very mosque, and will fight his substitute, the Evil One. This will be the Day of Judgment. There was no doubting the attentive devotion of these Muslim men, a devotion willing and unforced, a devotion which is daily increasing throughout the modern world.

We drifted slowly back into the courtyard, the setting sun now playing on the marble pavement and turning it into pure gold. We were outsiders, strangers to this worship, but something of the beautiful peace of the place settled on us and subdued us.

Close by the mosque is the tomb of Saladin, enemy of the Crusaders. At school, we had thought of him as one of the 'baddies' of history, but here, he was a hero. He succeeded in doing something very difficult – uniting all Muslim nations against the Crusaders. He retook the Holy City of Jerusalem for Allah. He was a man of honour who was never known to break his word. Even his enemies had to admire his military genius, his strict sense of justice, his many acts of gallantry and his kindness. It's interesting that the great poet Dante consigned Mohammed to the eighth circle of Hell (there are nine circles), while he honours Saladin by placing him in Limbo among such virtuous pagans as Plato, Socrates and Homer. He had no personal wealth, he hated ostentation and his tastes were extremely simple. At the age of fifty-four, as he lay dying, worn out by his many battles, a Christian chronicler reports that he summoned his standard bearer and told him, 'You who have carried my standard in battle will now go round Damascus with a piece of rag from my shroud on your lance. Call out that the Monarch of the East has taken nothing with him to his tomb except this cloth!' He ordered an inscription to be placed on his tomb: 'O Allah, receive this soul and open unto him the gates of paradise, the last conquest for which he hoped.'

We found our way to his simple tomb, set in a garden of lemon trees. As we gazed at it, we honoured in our hearts one of the 'goodies' of history. It was strange to think that the famous Englishman, Laurence of Arabia, had also stood before this tomb in October 1918, he who had led an Arab crusade against the Turks and who paid homage to a man who had driven the Crusaders out of Jerusalem 750 years before.

For us, Damascus is forever associated with St Paul. It was on his way to Damascus to persecute Christians that he had his apocalyptic vision. We were shown the street called Straight and the wall over which he escaped in a basket. Were they authentic? I have always had trouble identifying Christian narratives with actual places. For me, they exist outside time and place, yet are still true.

As I wandered around the crowded narrow streets of the Old City, I noticed a small church hemmed in by other buildings, a church dedicated to St George. As I belong to the Church of St George in Belfast, I decided to go inside to pay my respects to that warrior saint who died in Palestine in 303. He became known in England as early as the seventh century, but his cult took on a new dimension during the Crusades. Richard I placed himself and his army under the protection of St George. He became the patron saint of soldiers and was the ideal of Christian chivalry. There is little, if any, devotion to him now in England. Still, it's curious that St George's Day, 23 April, happens to be the birthday and death day of England's greatest poet, William Shakespeare.

I stepped inside the church. It was so dark that for a few moments I could make out nothing. As my eyes adjusted to the dark, I saw a rich interior with icons and candles glowing before them. There was a cross on the altar. I felt at home. Though fascinated and impressed by all I had seen in Islam, here I was close to all that was familiar. I walked about. As I was about to kneel, a woman's voice called out to me. I looked for the source of the voice and saw an elderly woman, head covered by a scarf, officiously tidying and arranging the candles on the candle stand. I smiled. With a severe expression, she pointed to the icon of St George and said commandingly, 'Pray! Pray!' And I did.

Was it in Mallula or Seidnaya that I had an impressive lesson in visual history? We were taken to a small stone church. We looked around and admired its simple beauty. A priest called us to the altar. It was a plain stone, free-standing altar, covered with a pure white cloth. He leaned forward, removed the cloth and there, underneath, was a pagan altar! It had channels along the side to receive the blood of the sacrificed animal and a hole to allow the blood to run down into a receptacle below. When the Roman Emperor Constantine became Christian in the fourth century, he ordered all pagan altars in the Empire to be destroyed and Christian ones put up in their place. Of the ones which escaped, only two now remain and this was one of them.

Damascus faces east across the desert to the River Euphrates to Mecca beyond. We were now to cross that desert, an immense, desolate space between Damascus and Baghdad. For centuries, huge caravans of camels laden with perfumes, silks and spices from India and China had crossed this desert to the great cities of Damascus and Constantinople. As we travelled, we saw mirages of lakes, water spouts, dust clouds and miles of honey-coloured sand. We were as excited as children when we came upon a herd of camels, numbering a thousand, we were told, and a handsome young Arab who was herding them. He was dressed in a dazzling long, white garment and the red and white headdress that the Arabs wear so stylishly. He stopped to talk. The camels were his livelihood, he said. Such a splendid herd made him a rich man and he was about to marry. His bride must bring a big dowry to the union to merit such a man. Would he find such a bride? Of course, there would be no problem. He smiled, wished us well and went on his way across the seemingly endless desert. Now and again we caught sight of a cluster of black nomad tents, people still living their solitary life as they have done for centuries.

Our goal that day was the Euphrates, a river which rises in Turkey and flows through Syria, a long journey of 2,430 kilometres, and into the Persian Gulf. For much of the journey, it runs below steep mud embankments so that you see it only as you draw near. For two thousand years, the river was of great importance, for trade as well as a military frontier and as an invaluable means of irrigation in the desert. In the ninth and tenth centuries, the Arabs allowed the waterwheels and irrigation canals to fall into disuse, and the Mongols completed the destruction in the thirteenth century. The Euphrates became a wasted river. But all along that great highway, the ruins of tels and forts remain to speak of the activities of the past.

We had come to see the Euphrates and to look over the important sites – the ancient city of Mari which flourished for over a thousand years from 2500 BC and the Roman fortress of Dura Europus, the great border fortress of the Greco–Roman world. For mile after mile, we saw nothing but desert. Eventually we came to the small town of Deir El Zor and thought we had arrived at our destination for the night. We were amazed when the bus drove right through the town and out again into the desert. After about five miles, we drew up outside a fine hotel which stood right on the banks of the Euphrates. It stood alone, not a village or even a house in sight. When we entered the foyer, we were surprised to see how elegant it was, furnished with palms and plants and easy chairs. It was completely empty. We were the only ones to sit down to dinner that night in the handsome dining room. What was such a luxurious hotel doing in the middle of the desert? We learned that it had been built not for tourists like ourselves, but for oilmen who came here from all over the world to prospect for oil. When the price of oil fell below $20 a barrel, there was no money for research. All the oilmen had gone and left the hotel to people like ourselves. It was eerie to be in such a hotel, quite alone in the desert.

At dinner that evening, I felt the first pangs of travellers' sickness and knew I was in for a bad time. I retired to my bedroom, which was huge and luxurious, and noticed with alarm that the bathroom was far from the bed. I crept into bed, my head aching, my feet freezing and my stomach heaving. I had a very unpleasant night and by morning I knew I wouldn't be fit to travel with the others to those famous sites I so much wanted to see. The rest of the party departed after breakfast. I alternated shakily between the bed and the lavatory. Not a sound reached me. I soon began to feel strangely alone. I crept to the window and looked out at the Euphrates, a broad and undistinguished expanse of water with no one in sight. I got back into bed. I began to wonder when the others would return, *if* they would return. Could I, by some terrible misunderstanding, be left in the desert forever? This sickness was giving me fantasies. Hours went by. Not a sound broke the silence. I lifted the phone and dialled reception. The telephone rang and rang. No response. I began to be really alarmed. I must somehow get downstairs and see what was going on. Shakily, I got myself dressed and pushed my belongings into my suitcase. That effort left me so weak I had to sit on the floor by the door to recover. I managed to get to the lift and down to the foyer. I sank into the nearest chair. There was no one in sight. Panic seized me. I now had the distinct impression that I had been abandoned. The fantasy was getting more and more real. Where was the receptionist? The staff? Humankind? I was longing for water to settle my thirst, but weakness kept me stuck to my chair. The hotel echoed with emptiness and outside was the limitless desert …

Just as I was on the point of screaming, a vehicle drew up outside. A rowdy party of my fellow travellers came through the front door together with our guide. He rang the bell. Immediately, a receptionist appeared from nowhere and the hotel sprang into action. The hotel staff, knowing that the whole party would be absent until mid-afternoon, had gone away, gone home, disappeared. They didn't know that one of the party had remained behind, sick in bed. Only in the desert was it possible to leave all doors open and unlocked and no security staff on duty! I was so relieved to see them all that I nearly cried with weakness and relief. I had missed Mari and Duro, but I was safe. I tottered into the bus and sat hunched, cold and sick as we continued our journey across the desert to Palmyra. By the time we reached it, I was beginning to feel better.

It's worth travelling to Syria just to see Palmyra. It must be one of the most romantic ruined cities in the world. To view the ruins of what was once a magnificent and prosperous city is always awesome, but to see it rising from the desert sands without a house or village in sight is unique.

The first view as you approach is of a huge city – streets, colonnades, temples, pillars, marketplaces, palaces – all strangely silent and empty. Agatha Christie, who travelled with her archaeologist husband Max Mallowan, described Palmyra in her wonderful autobiography, *Come Tell Me How You Live*, with 'its slender beauty rising up fantastically in the middle of the hot sand. It is lovely and fantastic and unbelievable, with all the theatrical implausibility of a dream.' It was the utter emptiness of it all which struck me – here is where people had walked about, done business, made plans, got married, given birth and died, and now here we were, alive and walking where once they had walked. Soon we, too, would be gone and others would come in their turn to exclaim and admire and wonder.

Palmyra was once a great city, even a grandiose one. It grew up beside an oasis where caravans of men and camels arriving from Persia and India and beyond were glad to rest after the heat and exhaustion of the journey. The Palmyrans did good business with them. Bigger business came along. The Romans were fighting the Parthians (Persians) who faced them on the other side of the Euphrates. Between the armies was a vast expanse of desert, made dangerous by marauding bandits. The Palmyrans organised a camel corps to police the desert and establish a secure route between the Roman fortress at Dura Europus and Homa in modern Syria. This operation made them very wealthy, and with this wealth they built beautiful buildings in their city. They invited the Emperor Hadrian to visit the city. He stayed for three weeks and to show his appreciation, he granted them free city status within the Empire. This entitled them to impose their own taxes. We know exactly what these taxes were, for a tablet was discovered on which was inscribed the whole tax system. They taxed donkeys, camels, goods, water, slaves: 'For the slave who is sold in town but who is not sent away, twelve denarii. For a senior slave who is sold, ten denarii.' Even prostitutes had to pay a monthly tax.

Within a hundred years, the city had become truly magnificent. With sublime hubris, the king of Palmyra, Odinat, called himself 'king of kings'. Within a few years, in 267, he was murdered in mysterious circumstances. His queen, Zenobia, was suspected of the murder. She was an extraordinary woman. Gibbon, in his *Decline and Fall of the Roman Empire*, said of her: 'She equalled in beauty her ancestor Cleopatra and far surpassed that princess in chastity and valour.' Zenobia was esteemed the most lovely as well as the most heroic of her sex. She was said to have pale skin, black eyes and white teeth. She was also intelligent and cultivated, attracting philosophers to her court. She was even more ambitious than her husband. She declared herself Augusta and her son Augustus and went as far as to lay claim to the eastern half of the Roman Empire. She led her armies against Rome, into Egypt and into Asia Minor. These military adventures were too much for Rome. The Emperor Aurelian, a seasoned soldier, marched against her and defeated her armies. Zenobia fled by camel across the desert, but was captured as she tried to cross the Euphrates. Aurelian brought her back to Rome in chains of gold. Her ancestor, Cleopatra, had killed herself rather than face this humiliation. When the Roman Senate mocked Aurelian for his victory over a mere woman, he is said to have replied, 'Ah, if you only knew what a woman I have been fighting! And what would history say if I had been defeated?' How did this extraordinary woman end her days? Some say it was in a villa in Tivoli, near Rome, surely an anti-climax.

Within months of Aurelian's departure from Palmyra, the citizens rose and murdered the Roman garrison. At this news, Aurelian hurried back and took full revenge, murdering the people and looting the city. The glory that was Palmyra was over.

We stayed the night in the small Hotel Zenobia in the middle of the ruins so that we could see them at their most beautiful, at dusk and dawn. After dinner, we sat outside on the terrace, en-thralled, watching the light fade on the empty city, on the backdrop of mountains and on the Arab castle perched so theatrically on top of one of these, the colours changing into ethereal shades of mauve and rose, then into azure blue and finally into indigo. The sands of the desert gleamed silver grey, then dark grey and black. The mass of the palm trees of the oasis nearby bent and sighed in the light wind. Then there was silence and we were alone with the past.

# Post-Glasnost Petersburg

## 2002

It would be extremely interesting to see St Petersburg after the fall of communism. There were now many more literary museums open, especially that of the poetess, Anna Akhmatova.

It's been twenty-six years since I first visited the USSR. That was a dramatic venture behind the Iron Curtain. Twenty-six years later, glasnost and perestroika have burst upon a moribund and corrupt society – the USSR has broken up and Russia has shrunk to a federation with millions of Russians living outside the national territory. Ukraine has become an independent republic, as have Georgia, Armenia and the countries of Central Asia. The Bolshevik Revolution of 1917 is now history. A tremendous restructuring is now going on. What I saw in 2002 was an extraordinary reversal of my first experience. No longer must one studiously avoid any mention of Lenin, Stalin, gulags and dissident writers. In fact, the guide said it all for us – Stalin was a brutal dictator, Lenin a cruel man and the *Aurora*, prized announcer of the Bolshevik Revolution, was now the boat that had delivered them into seventy years of slavery. Yet things were now much worse than they had been under the Soviets and there was wholesale corruption at all levels. When the state-owned factories were privatised, fortunes were made. Vouchers were issued to the workers which they didn't know were worthless. They sold the vouchers back to the factory owner for next to nothing. He then became the sole owner of the factory and sold off the stock and put the profits into dollar accounts abroad. It had all happened so quickly. People were confused. Yes, apartments previously rented from the state had been given to the owners, but some had big apartments and others had small ones. 'We are like people who have been a long time standing on the jetty. Someone pushed us into the water and we do not know how to swim,' our guide tells us. Advertisements invite you to consult doctors and dentists with 'Western standards' and the shops are full. But after all the years of subservience to the state, the salespeople don't know how to handle real customers. They are grudging, even sulky, their way, I'm told, of showing that they are just as good as these rich, patronising Western tourists.

We're staying in the same hotel as in 1974. It's still drab, but there are now curtains on the windows and there are no obvious spies in the foyer. The *Aurora* is still anchored in front of the College of the Naval Cadets – it will not completely disappear from view all through these White Nights of June opposite our hotel. The courtyard of the Alexander Nevsky Monastery is filled with beggars, many limbless; begging was a crime under the

Soviets. The Kazan Cathedral is no longer the Museum of Atheism, but the Museum of Religions. Workers from the provinces form a queue where they hope to be taken on as construction workers. This is a new concept, as labour was not for sale under the Soviet regime.

The supremely beautiful, slender spire of the Peter and Paul Church still reaches up to heaven, gold and ethereal, icon of mercy in that merciless fortress. I visit it again. The names of some of the famous men who have been incarcerated here, including Dostoevsky and Trotsky, are still over the doors of the cells. In the terrible Russian winter, there was only one small stove for two cells. I looked into a very sad cell where a woman had been imprisoned. One small window gave light from the outside world. Pigeons came to be fed at this window, a vital link with the living world outside. The authorities found out and put bars on the window. Unable to bear it, the woman set fire to herself from a small oil lamp in her cell. The authorities changed the lighting system from oil to electricity.

This year, the house of Anna Akhmatova, poetess, whom I love and admire, is open to the public. She, along with Marina Tsvetaeva and Osip Mandelstam, is among the greatest poets of the twentieth century. Little known outside Russia, she is well known and loved within it. She was strikingly beautiful, passionate and intelligent, and it was her fate to be caught up in all the turmoil of

her country in the twentieth century. She lived
from 1889 until 1965. Her first husband, the poet
Gumilyov, was shot in 1921 and two subsequent
marriages were unhappy. Her son and many of her
friends were sent to the gulags. 'Shakespeare's
plays,' she said, 'are mere child's play to the life of
each one of us.' She was persecuted and isolated.
Life was turned upside down during the Revolution: 'We aged a hundred years and this happened
in a single hour.' She refused to leave Leningrad
during the siege: 'I am not one of those who have
left my country to the mercy of its enemies.' Along
with hundreds of other women, she queued up
outside the prison in Leningrad, endlessly waiting
for the small window to be opened for news of
their loved ones and for permission to send
parcels. One woman, her lips blue with cold, whispered, 'Can you describe this?' 'I can', she said.
From this came her great sequence *Requiem*, which
expresses a new understanding of the Crucifixion
in Russian terms. The poems are the voice of all
the women everywhere who are forced to helplessly look on suffering. Akhmatova died in 1965,
but it took another twenty-five years before her
name could be spoken aloud. Now I could ask
about her, see where she lived and where she suffered.

I found my way to her apartment in the
Fontanka House. There, on the large landing, a
man had been perpetually posted to spy on her.
There is the room in which she was metaphorically

gagged and bound. There is her chaise longue from which she served tea to her visitors and, knowing her rooms were bugged, made coded conversation while passing her poems around. The visitors learned them by heart. She then destroyed them. The rooms are full of her presence – stylish, lion-hearted, determined to survive and to express in powerful words and rhythms what was happening to her country.

Valentina came to visit me today. Like Natasha, she had been a Russian language assistant in the Russian Department of Queen's University for two years. I welcomed her in Belfast, took her about and showed her some of the country. She had an aggressive manner, was quick to take offence and generally had to be handled with delicacy. I had kept in touch with her after she returned to Leningrad, her native city. During the winter before my arrival in 2002, she'd had pneumonia and had to go into hospital, a dangerous thing to do in Russia: 'It is preferable to die at home.' Her husband was responsible for finding and paying for the drugs which cured her. Without money, you didn't get better, she assured me. When she arrived at my hotel, she was looking as well and vigorous as ever, hair coloured too black to be flattering to her pale complexion, but neatly and becomingly dressed. She arrived in a flurry of red roses, the lovely way Russians have of greeting friends. Valentina wanted me to know that the Petersburg I was visiting was not the 'real' Petersburg.

She would take me to her apartment in the 'suburbs' so that I could see how a lecturer in English lived.

We meet the next day at my hotel. She wants to tell me how dreadful the long years under the communists were. I remembered how, in Belfast, during the Soviet years, she had ardently defended that regime. 'Why were you so vehement?' I asked.

'Well, when you are out of your country, you are always a patriot!' she replied. She had no car, as she couldn't afford one. 'How shall we get to your place?' I asked.

'Follow me and watch!' she answered in her usual determined manner. She stepped out onto the road and started to flag down passing cars. 'Every car here doubles as a taxi. That way, they can pay for the petrol.' The first car passed without stopping. The second car stopped. 'Don't speak,' she warned me. 'If he knows you're a tourist, he'll charge us double the price!' She negotiated and we climbed into the back seat. A stout man, smelling strongly of drink, occupied the passenger seat in the front. Was he a paying passenger too? As we started down a broad highway, the front passenger started to argue with the driver. He shouted, gesticulated, got almost violent so that the driver had difficulty keeping his eye on the road. I grew apprehensive. 'What's going on, Valentina? Are we safe?'

'Don't worry! Trust me.' I didn't. The driver cut dangerously across the traffic and drew up at the side of the road. He ordered the man out. He refused to move, whereupon the driver got out, went around to the passenger seat and threw the man out onto the pavement. I wanted to get out myself. 'Stay still and don't speak,' Valentina ordered. 'This thing is common. Everyone here drinks vodka, even in the morning.' We started up again and continued for several miles down the broad highway. The car started to make strange noises. Were the wheels going to fall off? These Russian machines are never properly maintained. With a succession of jolts, the car came to a stop in the middle of the road – we could be run into from behind at any moment. I pleaded with Valentina to get out. She was adamant. The driver looked puzzled, but finally got out of the car and, in the middle of the wide motorway, started to flag down passing cars. Very soon, a car did stop, the men negotiated and a tow rope was produced. We were linked up and were soon off again behind the rope, jerking and clanking for another five or six miles.

We drew up outside a huge complex of apartment blocks in 'brutal' style, put up by Stalin after the war to house the homeless. At the entrance to Valentina's block, young men lounged about and smoked. There was graffiti everywhere. 'That never happened under the Soviets,' Valentina said. 'Now, nobody cares any more.' We stepped into the lift, which looked as if it was about to disintegrate. I knew I was living very dangerously! We got out at the fourteenth floor. The flat had three small rooms – a living room with a huge TV screen, kitchen, bedroom and bathroom. Her husband had just arrived back from his *dacha* outside town. He had brought lettuce, onions and tomatoes which he had grown himself. He makes the long journey to the *dacha* by bus three or four times a week. Nearly everyone has a *dacha*. They range from shed-like structures to three-roomed centrally heated houses. We three sat down to table to a scanty meal. Vodka was poured and toasts proposed. The husband had spent many years working in Germany, so we conversed as best we could in German. 'He's a good man,' said Valentina. 'My first husband was a drunk.' Herbal pills were then distributed: 'Much better than any medicines you can get in Russia!' I wondered what they were for.

Valentina teaches now as a freelancer. 'I rent a room in town and take my pupils there. Everyone wants to learn English now. I want you to meet one of my pupils. He is a successful businessman. He imports kitchens from Sweden and installs them himself. He hopes to have them made in Russia soon. Tomorrow he will call for you at your hotel and he will take us both into the country, in the forest near the Gulf of Finland where Akhmatova is buried.'

The next day, he duly arrives in a four-wheel drive, accompanied by his son, a boy of about ten. This boy, it transpires, wants to come to Ireland to learn English. Could I arrange it? On the way to the forest, we stop at a large establishment. We are taken to a huge stable where horses are being groomed by stable boys. The businessman keeps two thoroughbreds here. We wait while the son gets on his horse and shows us how well he can ride. This is one of Russia's new capitalists. We stop briefly again at his country *dacha*, which is large and fenced off. I'm not invited inside. Eventually we get to the forest and walk towards a simple, plain grave, that of the beloved Akhmatova.

'Akhmatova loved this forest, and during her last years she spent each summer here,' said Valentina. 'Russians like to be buried in the forest.' She who had so little rest under Stalin now rests in peace. Tributes of red roses were scattered on her simple grave. I bowed my head before her, before her courage and the genius of her poems.

# Moscow

## *2002*

I made another visit to Moscow in 2002, and this time, my old friend Natasha came to see me in my hotel. Glasnost had caused the old paranoid taboos to come crashing down. 'How are things with you now, Natasha?' I asked.

'Very well, very well indeed. I am still teaching at the university and taking private pupils as well. Everyone wants to learn English!' Her chief concern at the moment was her daughter, Marina. Her husband, Kolya, had turned out to be 'no good' – he drank too much and didn't work. Many men are 'no good' in Russia, dying young from drink. Vodka was cheap and the production was state owned. Some people said that the government wanted to poison their own people. Women in Russia spoiled the men and made them unfit to be husbands and fathers.

Natasha had to take out a loan to pay off Kolya to get rid of him and they'd had to find him a place to live. All that had cost money which they didn't have. Marina had now got a job as a saleswoman in a shop, a job that didn't come up to her qualifications, but she was glad of it. Her only worry was having to come home late at night alone. A woman was very vulnerable in Russia these days – no strict Soviet law protected her. There were thieves and thugs everywhere. What could they do? You could trust no one. 'Only my family can be trusted. I live and work only for them. It is a pity. Society should be able to offer better than that. Still, there is no going back now …'

I'm astonished at the change in Red Square when I go there with Natasha. What lights! What colour! What détente! The Kremlin building and the History Museum are beautifully illuminated and the GUM store blazes with lighted windows displaying the latest fashions from Paris, London and Rome. The yellow and white of the Presidential Building in the Kremlin no longer terrifies. St Basil's has reclaimed its full glory, its gorgeous domes and cupolas, multicoloured zigzags of delight, the incarnation of every fairytale we have ever read. Couples stroll arm in arm in the warm evening air. Girls are in jeans and wear blonde hair, while boys are in jeans and sweaters with smart Western logos embroidered on them. This leisurely strolling is an entirely new concept.

Natasha tells me, 'Edith, I have a new God!' I knew she hadn't lost her old one throughout all the years of suffering, for she had drawn two small silver religious medals out of the interior of her purse, saying, 'I have kept them always with me.'

'Who is your new God?' I ask, curious.

'It is Luzkov, our Lord Mayor. He has made us

proud of our city. He went to the West and saw how cities were beautified there and he did the same for us here in Moscow. He even had this beautiful new cathedral built because the communists had blown up the old one. He appealed to ordinary Russians citizens to contribute to the rebuilding fund, and the whole sum was found, from a few roubles to millions.'

There are buskers everywhere plying their trade – an octet of classical musicians, a young virtuoso boy of about ten playing his violin like a Menuhin, a juggler. In contrast, old women, pitifully dressed, offer a few objects for sale. They were much better off under the Soviet regime; they are too old for the New Russia. Lenin's mausoleum is no longer the sacrosanct place it was when long queues waited to see their great leader. Now it's closed for the evening and two security guards stand relaxed outside the entrance. They are chewing gum. The Emperor has no clothes.

It's Friday evening. The roads, once empty, are now jammed with Ladas, which are £3,000 each. Horns are hooted furiously and traffic police try to control them. A wrecked car has been attached to a lamp post as a warning to careless drivers. Smart new apartments are being constructed for the 'new' Russians, whose wives stroll along the boulevards with pedigree dogs on leads.

Although the Soviets always promoted local authors, writers' museums and so on, they were careful to avoid anyone the regime didn't approve of. Glasnost has brought many of these victims back into favour and many more museums have been opened. Now Gorky's home as well as that of the poetess Marina Tsvetaeva, both victims of the Stalinist years, have been opened in Moscow.

Maxim Gorky is a name well known in the West. We aren't sure what became of him, but his early life was spent in squalor and violence. At four years of age, he was sent out into the world to fend for himself. He worked, among other things, as a dishwasher on a Volga paddle steamer, where he saw life in the raw. He devoured books and, strangely, found a trunkful of books belonging to the rough cook on board the steamer. He read the classics of Russian literature aloud to illiterate men and moved them to tears. It was his innate optimism and iron will which brought him through these years, years which he records in his famous trilogy. These experiences gave him a burning passion for justice for the poor – communism seemed to be the political solution which would bring it into being.

He was fêted by Stalin and gifts were loaded on him, such as a house in the Crimea, and his native town was renamed Gorky. Stalin knew what a gift such a talented writer was to his propaganda war. He made him a present of a magnificent art nouveau house in Moscow, the Ryabushinksy House, in 1931. It was close enough to the Kremlin for Stalin to keep an eye on him. In itself, the house is magnificent, with a wonderful stone staircase in the shape of a wave and stained glass windows in art nouveau designs. His study is sober; there was his large green desk, his spectacles, his pen, his books and his invisible presence. What went on in his head in those last years? His idols must have revealed their feet of clay. Did he close his eyes to what was going on around him? Did he ignore the letters he received from loyal Soviet citizens who had fled abroad? The Party wanted to ensure that Gorky did *not* know what was really going on. The newspaper *Pravda* was sometimes censored and an especially doctored copy printed and delivered to his house. He became a sort of prisoner in his own house, a broken man isolated from reality, or perhaps knowing all too much about it. Did he revolt in the end? The guide assured us that he was killed on Stalin's orders, probably poisoned. What could the beauty of art nouveau rooms do for a man who had been thus betrayed? The guide assured us that he never liked the house.

The poetess Marina Tsvetaeva is little known in the West. Even in translation, her poems are powerful and moving, with the disconcerting honesty, conversational style and dramatic intensity of Emily Dickinson. Her life story is pure nightmare. Her tragic presence and her poems haunt the large, airy rooms of her apartment, now open to the public, where she spent some happy years with her husband and children and wrote some of her finest poems. Then the nightmare began.

The years following the 1917 Revolution were years of terrible suffering for millions. Her husband, the writer Sergey Efron, joined the White Army and disappeared from home for almost five years. Marina Tsvetaeva was not a domesticated woman and her efforts to eke out a living during the Civil War were often fruitless. Four of the rooms of her apartment were taken over by other people and her furniture sold. There was no heat. The stairs were dark and cold, the banisters did not go all the way down and there were three treacherous steps at the bottom. 'The dark and cold came in from the street as if they owned the place,' wrote a friend. Such was her situation that she was obliged to place her two daughters in an orphanage, where one of them died of starvation in 1920, aged three years. Tsvetaeva left Russia for Paris in 1922 and began a long period of poverty and isolation. She became dependent on émigrés who first helped and then rejected her. Her husband changed his political affiliation and became a communist and worked as a Soviet agent. He went back to Russia in 1937 and was soon followed by his daughter.

Tsvetaeva, now alone, had to struggle to survive. Two years later, she, too, went back to Russia, where she discovered that her husband had been shot and her daughter sent to a labour camp. Pasternak befriended her, but he wasn't allowed to take in 'an enemy of the people'. She left Moscow with her son for a small town some six hundred miles east of the capital where others fed her. She hanged herself in 1941. No one attended her funeral and she was buried in an unmarked grave. Her son was later killed during the war.

The last time we made the journey from Moscow to Tolstoy's house in Yasnaya Polyana in 1984, some one hundred miles south of Moscow, there was snow on the ground. I can still shut my eyes and see the bark of the birch trees, the blanched white of the peeling bark against the tan of the trunks and the denser white of the snow. Then, there was little traffic and we bumped along a road full of ruts and potholes. Now, the highway has been repaired but is thronged with cars and it takes us a full four hours to get there. The summer pastures on either side of the road are rich with wild flowers, Queen Anne's lace, speedwell and buttercups and the full-leaved birches make an exquisite tracery of light and shadow on the ground. All around the house are orchards which Tolstoy planted himself; he loved working with peasants on the land. At the end of a long, shadow-filled drive is Volkonsky House, a long white building with an open-air wooden balcony where the family sat. I wonder again at the spaces the great man occupied, where his huge imagination created scenes and characters of extraordinary power. There is the living room with the children's corner, and at the other end, the conversation corner. Beyond is his beloved aunt's room from whom he learned the old ways of Russia. Then, his study, his books. At eighty-two, he was learning Japanese. We walk through the wood to where he is buried in an unmarked grave of green grass.

Tolstoy had tried to live as his conscience ordained. All his life, he was in search of God. God, he believed, was here on earth in the possibility of human goodness exemplified in the precepts of Jesus Christ. The Holy Synod had excommunicated him for his criticisms of the institutional church. After his death at the stationmaster's house at a country railway station where he'd fallen ill, the Church refused to say prayers for him. The railwaymen decorated his deathbed with juniper branches and placed a wreath 'To the Apostle of Love'. Another wreath made of paper flowers was cut out by the children. A peasant woman said to her son, 'Remember him, he lived for us.' The people started to chant the mass for the dead. The police in the next room, who had been instructed by the Holy Synod to make sure that this did not happen, rushed in with their swords by their sides. Everyone fell silent, but the singing was resumed, timidly at first. The government gave orders that the number of spectators was to be controlled in case of riots. A sculptor modelled his death mask and a painter, Mr Pasternak from Moscow, came with his son Boris, the future writer, to make a sketch.

Tolstoy's body was finally taken in a simple coffin to this place in the forest, where his brother

Nicolenko used to say the secret of universal love lay buried, engraved on a little green slab. Although it was the first public burial in Russia that wasn't attended by a priest, it was attended by thousands of his ardent admirers.

# Antioch

## *2002*

Antioch, famous city of antiquity and the Bible. It was here that the disciples first called themselves Christians.

We set out early in the morning from the big commercial port of Adana for the day-long journey to Antioch. As we passed through the rich cotton-growing plain called the Chukarova, the air grew hot and humid. The Chukarova is brought to life in the novels of Yesar Kemal. In *Memed my Hawk* (1955), he put into his pages the dreadful conditions for local women who harvested the cotton by hand. We read of the all-powerful and often cruel bosses, the Agas, who dominated the workers and often brutalised them with no redress from the law. Kemal, a famous writer, was born in the Chukarova in 1922. His father's forbears were well-to-do feudal lords, but his mother's family had been brigands. When he was five years old, Kemal saw his father brutally murdered while at prayer in a mosque. The shock caused him to develop a severe stammer which he was only free of when he sang. As a result, he improvised songs in the tradition of the Turkish minstrels and sang them himself. He laboured in the cotton fields and knew at first hand the hardships, the loyalties and the many sufferings of the peasants. He championed them all his life, and nowhere is his love for them better seen than in the fierce poetry of his novels. Now, fifty years later, the Chukarova has been irrigated, the rivers controlled and machines brought in to harvest the crop. We watched the huge machines at work where once the women toiled relentlessly.

In Turkey, you're never far from a fascinating historical site and, as we drove along the coast, past the Bay of Iskenderum, we came to the site of the Battle of Issus. It took place in 333 BC between Alexander the Great and Darius of Persia. The fighting was intense. Eventually, Alexander came face to face with Darius, whose chariot horses in battle were terrified by the noise, the smell of blood and the corpses. They plunged and reared. Darius transferred to another, lighter chariot and made off with Alexander after him. So close was the chase that Darius had to jump from his chariot and escape, jettisoning his armour and royal accoutrements as he fled on horseback, never slackening his pace, it was said, until he reached Babylon. He was, with his army, to live to fight another day.

Alexander came upon Darius' armour and brought it back to camp as a battle trophy. Alexander's soldiers celebrated their victory all night long. Alexander bathed in 'the Great King's tub' and adorned himself in 'the Great King's robe'. Suddenly, wailing was heard nearby. Darius' wife and mother were found sheltering in a tent, expecting to be killed at any moment. To their amazement, Alexander gave orders that they were to be treated honourably and were to retain all their titles, ceremonial adornments and insignia befitting their royal status. Alexander promised to bring up Darius' nine-year-old son with all the honours befitting his royal state. Alexander called him, and the child, not at all frightened, put his arms around the king's neck for a kiss. Alexander remarked, 'What a pity that the father lacked the son's courage and self-possession.' And on the plain at which we now gazed, a huge military funeral was held for the fallen, both Greeks and Persians, with Alexander's entire army on ceremonial parade.

As we left the Field of Issus behind us, the sky grew dark and overcast. Presently it began to rain heavily so that we could scarcely make out the Bay of Iskenderum on our right. We drove on through the rain, but as the bus reached the top of the pass which looks over the plain of Antioch, the skies suddenly cleared and we saw before us miles of flat, rich, fertile fields. It was the hinterland of Antioch, known as the Hatay, a land so rich as to have been the subject of a dispute between Turkey and its neighbour, Syria. At its heart was the rich trading city of Antioch, directly on the route between Asia and Europe.

As we drove along the road towards the city, the rain started again and was soon falling in torrents. In a few minutes, the road was a rush of floodwater six inches deep and, splashing and lurching, the bus picked its way through the water and pulled up outside our hotel. The street was crowded with people greeting each other loudly, buying and selling while the rain poured down. Our hotel was small, narrow and shabby, not the one that had been reserved for us, and the hallway was flooded with water. However, to be in Antioch was so exciting that we could easily put up with such discomforts. Tired by the excitements of the day, I fell gratefully into a hot bath and was pleasurably soaking away my fatigue when all the lights went out. Ten minutes later, I was still searching for my torch when there was a knock on the door. I opened it. A man's extended arm held a lighted candle. I could see neither his face nor body. Muslim courtesy, I said to myself as I reached for the candle. I headed downstairs for dinner and crossed by duckboards from the stairs to the dining room. The water was still flowing into the hall from the street and men and buckets seemed unable to stanch the flow. Everyone was cheerful. We ate a very good dinner that evening and greeted and talked with our Turkish neighbours as if floods were an everyday occurrence. As we ate and relaxed, the rain continued to fall and the excited bustle of the narrow streets outside drifted in. Nothing but an earthquake could keep a Turk from the real business of life.

The next morning, the rain was gone, the sun shone and the air was less hot and humid. Even the hallway was dry. We walked about the narrow streets of the old town among the pulsating mass of men, merchants, children and Mercedes cars. All life was lived in the street.

The Mosaic Museum is famous and its reputation is deserved. The pictures of fish, birds, lions, tigers, flowers, trees, gods and goddesses were rendered in mosaics with all the vividness, intensity and colour of a child's eye. In Roman times, many of the wealthy merchants who had made fortunes from the sale of perfume, soap and glass built large villas and paved them with these mosaics.

A quarter of an hour's journey took us to the suburb of Harbiye, set in a refreshing, cool gorge of waterfalls and oleander trees. It was called Daphne by the Greeks. Legend has it that the virgin Daphne, besieged by the persistent and unwanted attentions of the god Apollo, prayed to be delivered from him. Her prayer was answered – she was turned into a laurel tree and rooted forever in this beautiful place. She thus gave her name to our garden shrub. And it was here in Daphne that, quite inappropriately, Mark Antony chose to wed the very unvirginal Cleopatra in 40 BC.

Antioch had a special resonance for those of us who were brought up in a Christian culture. We had all heard of Antioch in the Bible. A large community of Jews was established in Antioch in the years when the first Apostles lived. It was in Antioch that the Apostle Peter fled from the wrath of the Jews of Jerusalem after the Crucifixion. He is said to have taken refuge in a nearby cave owned by St Luke the Evangelist who came from Antioch. Later, Paul and Barnabas joined Peter and it was there that the disciples were first called Christians. We all wanted to visit this cave-church. A quick phone call was made to a resident priest and a service was arranged for the group. 'Ah, you are Irish, you say? How interesting! I am an Italian. I spent a year there near Dublin!' His aquiline Italian features relaxed into a nostalgic smile as he remembered those days. 'So, you are from Northern Ireland? I never got there. Yes, yes, we have heard much about the bombings and killings that go on there. Is it really as bad as they say?'

'Yes, in many ways it is,' I answer, 'but here you see a group of thirty people, some Roman Catholic, some Protestant and some agnostic. We all get on together and for one reason or another want to attend a service in this special place.' Yes, he would conduct it, no trouble at all. He looked with new interest at this unusual group of people.

At the appointed time, we climbed up the steep slope to the mouth of the cave and went inside. It was bigger than I had expected. The walls were black with two centuries of candle smoke and water oozed from the rock. A small, simple altar and half a dozen rows of pews now occupied the space where Peter, Paul and Barnabas had once talked together. Peter had seen Jesus. A hush fell over our usually talkative group as we filed into the seats. Our Muslim guide, curious, sat at the back of the cave. The priest appeared, vested in a simple white garment. As leader of the group, I was appointed to read out the relevant passage from Scripture. This was much more than a reading of the Gospels in church on a Sunday morning. We were all aware of the uniqueness of the occasion.

'And the hand of the Lord was with them: and a great number believed, and turned unto the Lord.' A short, simple mass commenced, and when the time came, every member of the group lined up, hands outstretched, to receive the bread. We filed out, shook the priest by the hand and made our way back down the slope to the bus, conscious that something very special had taken place.

# Ukraine: The Steppe

## 2003

Ukraine is the native land of Joseph Conrad and the Crimea, the convalescent home of Tolstoy and Chekov, and Kiev, the heart of old Russia.

Steppe, savannah, tundra were three magical words in our geography class at school. I was confused as to which was which and in what country each was found, but as a lover of words, I loved these ones. They suggested vast, limitless areas unimaginable in an Ireland of little fields. How could one ever cross them? Later in my reading, I was to learn that the steppe was in Russia, and in Russian novels, people travelled across it in carriages mounted on skis, were bogged down in snowdrifts, were even lost for days on end in these endless flat spaces and sometimes even died.

Now, in the twenty-first century, it's possible to experience these immense plains in a comfortable manner by train or coach. The time was right in 2003 – tourism was now possible in this post-glasnost age. But what did we know of Ukraine? Very little. Now was the time to learn more of this marvellous, unfortunate and enduring country.

To the ordinary European, Ukraine is known, if at all, as a large, vague territory somewhere to the south of Moscow. To the Russians themselves, it's much more familiar. To them, it's part of their homeland, much as Scotland and Wales are thought of as part of the homeland of Great Britain. Yet today, after centuries of dependence, Ukraine is an independent republic with its own parliament, its own institutions, its own language. This state of affairs dates only from 1991, following the collapse of the Soviet Union, which Ukraine was an integral part of. In 2005, a parliamentary election had been fought, disputed, re-run and finally decided. A pro-Europe Yevtushenko survived poisoning and came out a winner as president of the country. Since then, he has had to sack his whole cabinet for corruption. The Ukraine is bitterly divided. What lies ahead?

The word 'Ukraine' means 'edge' or 'borderland', and although the country, which is slightly larger than France, is located wholly in Europe, its position next door to Asia and its rich black soil (its *chorezem*) has drawn invader after invader to its land over the centuries. Scythians and Mongols have come plundering from the east from the Asian steppe, and Norsemen came adventuring from the north; Norsemen and Vikings travelled as far as Ireland, but they also reached the Black Sea. A great trade route once ran from Scandinavia down the rivers Bug and Dnieper to the Black Sea and onward to the important trading city of Constantinople. Some of these adventurers decided to settle permanently on the Dnieper at a point where

Kiev now stands. There, they founded the city of Kiev and thrived. They were gradually assimilated into the culture of their Slavic subjects – names changed over time, becoming Slavicised. The Swedish Waldemar became Vladimir and Vladimir became king, coming to the throne of Kiev over a thousand years ago. The story of his conversion from paganism to Christianity is legendary.

Vladimir decided that his pagan subjects needed an 'advanced' religion. What should he choose? Emissaries were sent out to the Muslim Bulgars, but circumcision and abstinence from pork and wine did not appeal. Missions to Jews and to Catholic Germans also failed to attract: 'We saw them performing many ceremonies in their temples but we beheld no glory there.' But a mission to the great church of Hagia Sophia in Constantinople bowled them over: 'We knew not whether we were in heaven or upon earth. For on earth there is no such splendour and beauty and we were at a loss how to describe it. We only know that God dwells there among men and their services are fairer than the services of other nations.' Vladimir was converted. In 988 he obliged all his subjects to be baptised en masse in the river Dnieper. A man witnessed and left an account of that event: 'Some stood up to their necks, others to their chests, the younger nearer the bank, some of them holding children in their arms ... there was joy in heaven and upon earth to behold so many souls saved.'

Vladimir's son, Yaroslav the Wise, made Kiev
an important political and cultural centre. He built
the great cathedral of St Sophia in Kiev in imita-
tion of Hagia Sophia in Constantinople. By choos-
ing Christianity from Byzantium rather than from
Rome, Vladimir bound the future Russians, Belorussians and Ukrainians together in the Orthodox religion, thus dividing them from their
Catholic neighbours, the Poles, with ongoing consequences to this day.

Thus Kiev became the capital of the first Slavic
civilisation. From the tenth to the thirteenth century, it seems to have been regarded as the real
heart of Russian Orthodoxy. Under the tsars, pilgrims came in their thousands to worship at its
shrines. But during the next five hundred years, it
became a backwater as it was devastated again and
again. In the thirteenth century, Genghis Khan, in
his terrifying career from the Asian steppe to
Europe, never quite reached Kiev, but his son
Baku did. He swore 'to tie Kiev to my horse's tail'.
He devastated the city in 1242 and all but a handful
of its four hundred churches were burned. Only a
hundred and fifty years later, another Mongol,
Tamburlaine the Terrible, whose very name made
people tremble, smashed it again. When the Mongol army withdrew two years later, Kiev went into
a long decline. According to Russians, after the retreat of the Mongols, the population of Kievan
Rus migrated north, taking their culture and civilisation with them and Kiev was reborn in Moscow.

Ukrainians utterly deny this and claim that Kievan Rus remained Ukrainian.

From the fourteenth century to the middle of the seventeenth, by a vicissitude of history, present-day Ukraine was ruled by a Polish–Lithuanian alliance from its capital at Kraków. Their subsequent alliance with the Catholic Poles had endless consequences for Eastern European history. After the partition of Poland in 1793, much of Ukraine passed from Polish to Russian hands and during the following century the tsars encouraged Russians to emigrate to Ukraine, effectively making it a colony. In the eighteenth century, Empress Catherine the Great, passing through Ukraine on her way to view her newly expanded Empire, which had now reached the Black Sea, could hardly believe the poor state of Kiev, 'the new Jerusalem', 'the city of glory': 'From the time I arrived I have looked round for a city but so far have only found two fortresses and some outlying settlements.' Under her reign, Ukraine became an integral part of Russia and it remained so until the First World War, which saw the collapse of tsarist Russia and the success of the Bolshevik Revolution. Ukraine then had a chance to become independent, but because so many factions were competing for power, independence failed.

Stalin came to power in 1923. Then began the real horror. He set about taming this turbulent country and getting rid of 'harmful nationalism'. In the process, he committed terrible crimes against its people. In a country where food was abundant, he deliberately engineered a famine. In 1932 to 1933, he collectivised the farms and ordered farmers to produce unrealistic quotas of grain. The harvest was entirely confiscated and terrible measures taken against the starving peasants. House-to-house searches were enforced, watchtowers were set up in fields and people starved to death in their thousands. Any woman or child caught stealing grain could be killed. Entire villages died of starvation. Even cannibalism took place, such was the desperation of the people.

The cities of Ukraine suffered as well as the country. Intellectuals and dissidents were transported to labour camps in Siberia. Cathedrals and palaces were razed to the ground and whole villages deliberately destroyed. The infamous famine killed more people than all those killed in the First World War. But that was not the end of the people's suffering. In 1939 came the Second World War, which brought unparalleled violence and destruction to Ukraine. Nearly 5.5 million were killed, or one in six of the entire population.

Of course, Ukraine wasn't the only nation to suffer in this way. Richard Overy, historian, says: 'Across a vast no man's land from the Baltic states in the north to the shores of the Black Sea in the south was played out a human tragedy that still defies imagination. The population of Belorussians, Ukrainians and Jews was caught up in a drama not of their making' – caught between the Nazis and the Red Army. In September 1939, the German army marched into Poland from the west. Two weeks later, the Red Army did the same from the east. By mid-October, Poland was wiped off the map. On 21 June 1941, the Germans attacked the USSR and marched into Ukraine. Kiev fell in mid-September, Odessa in October, Sevastopol in 1942. The German army was to occupy Ukraine for nearly two years.

At first, many Ukrainians welcomed the Germans, thinking that they would free them from the Soviet yoke, but to the Nazis, they were merely Slavs, *untermenschen*, vermin to be eradicated. Once conquered, Ukraine was to be the eastern half of the Thousand-Year Reich. Mass deportations took place of Ukrainian citizens to Germany as slave labour. Most Ukrainian cities were destroyed and the economy ruined. Shocking things were done, even painfully ridiculous ones – for instance, the entire Ukrainian football team was executed for having won several matches against German army teams.

In early 1944, the Red Army launched a massive counterattack and pushed the German army back west. In the process, most of what was left of Ukraine was destroyed. After the war ended, Ukraine came again under the Soviet umbrella. During the Cold War, little more was heard of it until the Chernobyl disaster shocked the world and the terrible state of the Soviet infrastructure was revealed, as large areas suffered lethal doses of radiation.

I was returning from a visit to Cuba in the late 1980s on an Aeroflot aeroplane, which was making a stop at Shannon. The plane left Havana two hours later than was scheduled. As is usual in communist countries, no reason was given for the delay. Then a hundred or more pale, thin children appeared, walking hand in hand in line. They were boarded onto the plane, each clutching a basket of fruit. They were Ukrainian children returning from a session in Cuba's good hospitals, children who had been in the radiation field of Chernobyl. They looked pale, ill and unhappy.

In 2003, I persuaded seven other adventurous women to accompany me on a visit to Ukraine. We flew direct from London to Kiev. After the devastation of two world wars, we were surprised to find Kiev a very fine city. It had been rebuilt by the Soviets, and like all Soviet planned cities, it was on a grand scale with its huge city squares, immense public buildings and, along the River Dnieper, broad boulevards thickly lined with trees, the 'green lungs' of the city of which they were inordinately proud. The main street, Kreshatik, is so wide and tree lined that it compares well with the Champs Elysées.

Amazingly, some old buildings from Kievan 'Rus' have survived. The St Sophia cathedral and monastery complex still stands. It's very beautiful, with its soaring Russian domes and gleaming gold crosses, which seem to float unanchored in the great bowl of the sky. Inside, it's richly decorated in magnificent Byzantine style. An exquisite iconostasis of long, slender saints draped in ochre and pink marches around the walls, while Christ, Pantocrator, stands in the main cupola and a massive Virgin in vivid blue glass mosaic on a deep gold ground looks down on the saints. An inscription taken from Hagia Sophia in Constantinople reads: 'God is in the midst of her, therefore she shall not be moved. God helps her from morning until morning.' How many troubled souls must have turned to her in supplication during the destroying centuries ... Orthodoxy is exquisitely visual and sensory. For the Orthodox, God, by becoming man, has, in a unique sense, conferred honour upon the material.

The most famous monastic site in Kiev is the Monastery of the Caves. Like thousands of pilgrims before us, we made our way there. It was founded in the eleventh century by hermit monks who established themselves along the Dnieper, digging themselves deeper and deeper into the earth as the years went by. Their dead bodies didn't decompose, which is taken as a sign of sainthood in Orthodoxy. At the entrance to the caves, we were each given a candle to light us through the dark, serpentine passages. We moved silently along in single file, heads bent to avoid the low roof. At intervals we came upon a monk's cell lit only by dim candles. A solemn, pale acolyte stood sentinel over the niche where the mummified body of one of the saints lay draped in red and green vestments in an open-topped glass coffin. The hushed and solemn religious atmosphere, the glow of the candles in the dark, the pale, dedicated young monks and the sense of timelessness all had a big effect on us. We felt that we were indeed in a holy place and were likewise hushed and silent.

We already knew something of Ukrainian writers, but there was a great deal more to know. As modern-day Western Ukraine had at one time been Polish, a writer like Conrad is a Ukrainian, although born in Terehovye eighty miles south-west of Kiev. His family name was Korzeniowski. His parents were fanatically patriotic. 'Tell yourself that you are without love, without Fatherland, without humanity as long as Poland, our mother, is enslaved,' his father said. He seems to have had an overdose of patriotism, for at sixteen years of age, he left home to join the French Merchant Navy and subsequently the British Merchant Navy. He only returned once to his home, preferring to settle in England.

Western Ukraine also produced a famous poet, Paul Celan, whose poem 'Todesfugue' is the most powerful of all poems on the Holocaust. Joseph Roth, the novelist, was from Polish-ruled Galicia. Both these men were Jews. Celan's parents were both killed by the Nazis; haunted by guilt, he threw himself into the Seine. Roth died a penniless alcoholic at a café table in Paris. The house-museum of Mikhail Bulgakov is in Kiev, whose novel, *The Master and Margarita*, a fantastical satire on Good and Evil in the days of Stalin, is well known in the West. His novel *The White Guard* was set in Kiev and describes the battle between the Whites, the Reds and Ukrainian partisans for his beloved city.

Bulgakov wrote of his native city: 'Beautiful in the frost and mist-covered hills above the Dnieper, the life of the city hummed and steamed like a many-layered honeycomb. All day long smoke spiralled in ribbons up the sky from innumerable chimneypots. A haze floated above the streets, the packed snow creaked underfoot; houses towered to five, six and even seven storeys. By day the windows were black, while at night they shone in rows against the deep dark-blue sky.' A cast-iron statue of St Vladimir holding an illuminated cross (still standing in Kiev) hovers over the action. As the Bolsheviks prepare to take the city from the partisans, Bulgakov turns the saint into a warrior 'turning the cross into a sharp and menacing sword'. For Bulgakov, Vladimir was defending a lost empire, a lost way of life, an identity.

Naturally, Bulgakov ran foul of Stalin. By 1929, all his plays had been banned. He wrote a letter to Stalin asking permission to leave the country: 'I am condemned to silence and quite possibly to complete starvation.' The response was a telephone call from Stalin himself: 'We have received your letter and read it with our comrades. You will have a pleasing answer. Perhaps we really should let you go abroad. What is it? Have we bored you so much? I have thought very much recently about whether a Russian writer can live outside his motherland. And it seems to me that he cannot.'

'You are right. I don't think so either.'

'Where do you want to work? At the Arts Theatre?'

'Yes, I would like to. But I asked about it. They refused me.'

'Well, submit a request there. It seems to me that they will agree ...'

We were taken to the house where he lived in Kiev. It was quite extraordinary. The White Guard had taken over. Everything in it – walls, doors, furniture, exhibits, the guide herself – were all in white. It was like viewing a landscape after a snowstorm.

So, we had come all the way from Ireland to see Bulgakov's house? How interesting! The guide was so enthusiastic, so voluble that she quite overwhelmed us with details. We were rare tourists, it seemed, and we gave her hope for her important work.

We couldn't be long in Ukraine without coming up against the story of Ukrainian anti-Semitism. The torment of the Jews reached its most terrible point in Ukraine after Hitler's armies invaded. The name Baby Yar will be forever written in letters of fire in the annals of that occupation. We had heard of it and wanted to see it. Just eight days after Kiev

surrendered on 27 September 1941, the Jews of
Kiev were rounded up by the Germans and taken
to a long ravine on the outskirts of the city called
Baby Yar. Men, women and children were driven
towards it in columns and ordered to stand on the
edge of the ravine. They were stripped, their valu-
ables taken, and then were shot in the back of the
head, falling forwards into the ravine. In forty-
eight hours of non-stop killings, 33,771 Jews were
dispatched by SS men and Ukrainian militiamen.
Soviet prisoners of war were also killed. The earth
which was shovelled into the ravine on top of the
corpses didn't stop moving for some time afterwards. Such noxious fumes arose from the pile that
Heydrich, head of Nazi security, ordered the bodies to be dug up and cremated.

I asked our guide if we might be taken to Baby
Yar. She answered coldly, 'We do not usually take
tourists to such places.' I knew what her tone
meant. Many Ukrainians had a very ambivalent at-
titude towards Jews. However, she reluctantly
agreed to take us there. We went by coach through
the town into a modern suburb. It was Sunday afternoon. Everything was peaceful. We looked for
the notorious ravine and saw not a deep precipice,
but a small wooded valley, part of a leisure park
where families were picnicking and children playing. Part of the original ravine had been filled in
and apartment blocks built on top, everything
providing a picture of happy, innocent living.
Nevertheless, we could see where the murderous

ditch was situated. A dramatic sculptural ensemble stood at the entrance to the park. It was erected in 1976 by the Soviet authorities to 'all those Soviet prisoners of war, soldiers, murdered here by the Nazis.' There was no specific mention of the Jews. It wasn't until 1991, after the fall of communism, that a smaller memorial in the shape of a menorah was erected closer to the actual site and specifically dedicated to the Jews. We gazed at the place in complete silence. The guide said nothing. I marvelled once more at how the waters cover even the bloodiest of deeds and life reasserts itself.

We were to make the long journey from Kiev to Sevastopol by train, my very favourite mode of transport. Kiev railway station had all the bustle and excitement we used to love at railway stations when we were children. It was thronged with people, suitcases, bags, bunches of flowers, talk, laughter, tears, embraces by those leaving and those who were being left behind. It was a scene of the most unselfconscious fellowship and cheerfulness, in which we eight tourists passed almost unnoticed. Our guide pushed her way through the crowds and we followed. She found our reserved sleepers and we jumped into the compartment and installed ourselves. What other transport equals the excitement of a night sleeper when, curled up on your bunks, villages and towns flash past and only the change in the darkness tells you of the outside world?

There were still fifteen minutes before the departure time. I jumped down from the high train and onto the quayside to mingle with the crowd and to view the peasant women who had come in from the country to sell their wares – wild mushrooms, strawberries, home-made yoghurt, tomatoes. I bought strawberries for our whole party at a negligible price and was just strolling about when a sharp voice called out to me. It was the guard of our compartment. She was about thirty years old, slim, blonde, pretty and very smart in her guard's uniform. She motioned me to get back up on the train, which I did. She was not a woman to argue with. She stood to attention on the platform beside her compartment, waved her flag, blew her whistle and jumped back onto the running board. We were off! She looked at us sternly as we hung out of the windows to see the station and the waving people pass. She was not going to be intimidated by 'rich' tourists.

As the train gathered speed and we eventually settled down, we could see her busying herself at a samovar at one end of the corridor. I smiled at her and said in my simple Russian, 'We all think you are very pretty!' At this, she started because she had been addressed in Russian and because of the compliment. A slight smile crossed her face, then the stern look reappeared. I managed to ask her about her life as a guard – how many days a week she worked, where she lived and about her husband and two children. She didn't encourage any more conversation, but that night, as we rolled through the Ukrainian steppe, she supplied us with endless cups of tea. For as long as the light lasted, we watched the flat countryside flash by – fields, villages, onion domes, farmyards, forests – until darkness fell and we could see no more. We pulled down the blinds, climbed into our bunks and fell asleep to the sweet, monotonous music of wheels on tracks.

The next morning, we arrived at Simferopol and were transferred at once to a minivan for the two-hour drive to Sevastopol. Sevastopol is forever associated in the British mind with the Crimean War, the Charge of the Light Brigade, Balaclava and Florence Nightingale. The whole area was top secret under the Soviets, and now, in 2003, it seemed strange and exciting to come upon it like this, alighting from a minivan, unsupervised, unwatched by hostile eyes. I realised that the Soviet suspicion I had known all over the Union was now a thing of the past. But I could understand how, for those who had lived through it, the fear of authority, of informers, would never go. Perhaps that hostile system would come back? One never knew.

During the Crimean War, both sides lost an estimated 250,000 men. In the Second World War, the German army made another onslaught on Sevastopol. They occupied the city for two hundred days, during which time the city lost nearly half its population. A fascinating surprise was to be brought to see the vast diorama which visually sets out, in three dimensions, the military front in the Crimean War. Though the diorama was destroyed in the Second World War, it had been rebuilt by the Soviets. From the viewing platform, the scenes in the diorama – the trenches, flags, guns, heaped bodies, dead and dying horses, gleaming bayonets – were very dramatic. Schoolchildren were being shepherded along by guides intent on making real the history of their town. They were all orderly and well behaved. They looked at us curiously, eight people who might have been schoolteachers come for a history lesson!

Apart from the famous war, Sevastopol is a holy city for Russian Orthodoxy. On the edge of the town lies the ruins of Chersonesus, the remains of a Greek city where the Byzantine missionaries Cyril and Methodius first landed in Russia, bringing the Gospel and the Cyrillic alphabet with them. We had to use our imaginations, though, as there was little to see.

The Crimea is now Ukrainian, although in 1991, when Gorbachev held a referendum on the maintenance of the Soviet Union, 88 per cent of Crimeans voted in favour of keeping the Union, the highest percentage of any city in Ukraine. It is now 66 per cent Russian speaking. Since independence, the Soviet Black Sea Fleet has been a bone of contention between Russia and Ukraine. Who owned it? After much wrangling, it was eventually split between both countries. No agreement could be reached as to the exact divisions until 1999, when Ukraine agreed to lease Sevastopol Port to Russia for twenty years in return for cancelling Ukraine's large oil debt to Russia.

On the glorious sunny morning we strolled along the famous waterfront, its military significance was signalled by the number of army and naval personnel moving about in a very relaxed manner, Russian officers wearing smart black and gold uniforms, sailors in bell-bottom trousers and brimless ribboned hats, while Ukrainian military personnel were in camouflage green. Shades of the imperial past looked at us from the great classical stone archway and steps leading down to the water where the Russian tsar came to view his fleet. Now children played innocently on the steps. The view out to sea was beautiful. We looked for evidence of the Black Sea Fleet but saw only a few rusting battleships resting at anchor. The big seagoing ships, we were told, were anchored in harbours along the coast.

Our next goal was Yalta. Such a beautiful peninsula as the Crimea, strategically hanging as it does into the Black Sea, has been fought over for centuries. Greeks occupied it, then the Tatars ruled it for five hundred years. The Russian Empire annexed it in 1788. The Russians tore down almost all reminders of the Tatar past, including hundreds of mosques and palaces. One of the few buildings to have survived intact is the Palace of Bakhchisaray, made famous in Pushkin's poem 'The Fountain of Bakhchisaray'. In 1944, Stalin deported the whole Tatar population from the Crimea to Central Asia and to Siberia, the excuse being that they were pro-Nazi. I remembered Atila, our Tatar guide in Istanbul in 1974; his people had been deported from the Crimea and had settled in Turkey. Their fate had left a deep wound. Since the late 1980s, about a quarter of a million Tatars here have been allowed to return, but they have not been easily assimilated.

As we travelled along the beautiful coast road from Sevastopol to Yalta, the mountains rose up steeply on our right, while on our left, the sea was the colour of pure lapis lazuli blue. Slim cypress trees, vines and terraces told us that we were now in a Mediterranean climate. Under the tsars, rich people came here for health and leisure. The tsar built himself a palace in Livadia, three kilometres west of Yalta. It was there that the famous Yalta Conference took place in February 1945 between Stalin, Roosevelt and Churchill. We were taken to see the table where the fateful carve-up of Europe was arranged. Under the Bolsheviks, however, Yalta was opened up to workers and their families. In December 1929, Lenin signed an order making Yalta a health resort for workers and filled the coastal plain with sanatoria.

Our destination in Yalta was the Hotel Yalta. Its situation, backed by high mountains and facing the sea, was superb. Its size, however, was out of keeping with the landscape. It was of truly Soviet dimensions – sixteen floors, ten bars, seven restaurants, many leisure amenities and a lift up and down to its own private beach. All our rooms faced the sea, so everyone was satisfied! We spent a lot of time exploring the complex and having a quick bathe in the Black Sea. In the evening, we went to the restaurant for dinner, but it was so vast, with so many tables and so many people, that we had difficulty finding the tables assigned to us. We eventually found our places right under the platform where a live orchestra was playing popular tunes. People all around us were eating, drinking, talking and laughing in truly festive mood, no Russian taciturnity about them! They paid no attention to us foreigners until I turned to the people at the table next to us, introduced myself, and asked what was going on.

Belfast? Yes, they had heard of Belfast. 'Bombs,' they said. They were puzzled as to why we had come all the way from Ireland to see Ukraine. They seldom saw foreign tourists. I learned that they were Ukrainians from all over Ukraine gathered here in Yalta for a weekend to celebrate the end of the football season, to give out trophies to the winning teams and generally to enjoy themselves. We were at once drawn into their circle, names exchanged, champagne and vodka liberally poured into our willing glasses. Then glasses were raised, toasts proposed to Ukraine, to football, to Ireland, to anything else we could think of. The atmosphere was warm, happy, unselfconscious. Ludmilla, my neighbour, is a short, squat woman with grey hair. She is a nurse, sixty-four years old, but has unbounded energy, she tells me. Her husband, Vladimir, is a radio engineer. They are passionately fond of football. As the band plays waltzes and foxtrots, our neighbours stretch out their hands to us – come and dance! We move about on the floor, dance after dance. There is no rowdiness or drunkenness. When the prizes are announced, team leader after team leader goes up to the platform to receive his trophy and to be vigorously applauded. More champagne, more laughter, more dancing. A slim young man with handsome, clean-cut features comes up to Anne, saying, 'May I introduce myself?', his formula for 'May I have the next dance?', and he uses it each time he asks her to dance. They look happy and relaxed as they turn and twirl. He is an air-controller from the Donetz industrial region with a wife and two children at home. The whole party is to leave Yalta the next morning to travel the long return journeys by coach to their separate destinations.

Around midnight, I slip away to bed, leaving Anne and the air-controller to dance until the small hours. They take a turn on the terrace to look at the sea. He is charming and dignified with her. Early the next morning, there's a discreet knock on our door. I open it. It's him! 'I have come to say goodbye,' he says and bows slightly. Anne, who's washing her hair, emerges dripping and embarrassed from the bathroom. He takes her hand, then mine. 'Goodbye. Goodbye.' And he turns away. It was a brief encounter of the happy kind.

Not only tsars and nobles came to Yalta, but writers too. The great Leo Tolstoy, aged and sick, came here to recover his health and stayed ten months at a lovely house belonging to Countess Panin at nearby Gaspra. At that time, he was famous and admired but had been excommunicated by the Orthodox Church for his many unorthodox views and he was even trailed by government spies. When he was at death's door, his wife Sonya received a letter from the Metropolitan Anthony exhorting her to reconcile her husband to the Church. But for Tolstoy, there was no reconciliation possible. A photo shows him in bed, thin and haggard. He very nearly died, first of pneumonia, then of typhus, but was nursed back to health by his devoted but exhausted wife.

This house was nationalised by the Bolsheviks in 1921. Now, nearly a hundred years later, we were free to wander through its rooms and roam in its beautiful garden full of exotic trees and magnificent statuary. The house is now a sanatorium for children with chronic chest disorders. The medical equipment in the rooms looked out of date. We could see mothers with pale children wandering aimlessly in the gardens. The state, we learned, helped pay for their stay with a system of vouchers.

Another writer who spent time in Yalta was Anton Chekhov. He, too, was in poor health as he battled against consumption. The mild climate of Yalta kept him more or less a prisoner there most of the last five years of his life.

The two great writers, both ailing, visited each other. Chekhov saw how much Tolstoy had aged: 'The worst disaster is age which has now affected him completely,' he wrote to the writer Maxim Gorky. Tolstoy didn't like Chekhov's plays: 'Shakespeare's plays are bad enough, but yours are even worse,' he told him. He didn't like his 'materialistic' views. 'Chekhov is not a spiritual man,' he declared.

Chekhov seems to have kept his temper. He loved and revered Tolstoy as a writer. 'I have loved no man as I have loved him ... When there is a Tolstoy in the world of literature, it becomes a fine and easy thing to become a man of letters,' he wrote. Here, where we stood on the terrace at Gaspra, looking over the sea, the two men had long talks together, Chekhov dressed like a schoolteacher, with his dangling eye-glass and hollow chest, and Tolstoy in his peasant blouse and long, flowing white beard, talking, talking. Tolstoy liked Chekhov: 'He has an atheist's heart, but a heart of gold.'

Yet another famous writer stayed nearby – Maxim Gorky, exiled to the Crimea for his Marxist opinions. He was a real man of the people, unlike the other two. He had had a cruel and impoverished upbringing, which he records in *My Childhood*, had run away from home and plied every trade under the sun. The injustices he saw and suffered had made him a Marxist. As I stood on the terrace, I thought of the three men talking here together: the nobleman, Tolstoy, dressed as a peasant and aspiring to be one; the professional doctor, Chekhov; and the true peasant, Gorky, all debating Tolstoy's advanced ideas.

'Why don't you believe in God?' asks Tolstoy.

'I have no faith,' answers Gorky.

'That's not true. By nature you are a believer, you cannot live without God ... you must tell yourself "I believe" and everything will be all right.'

'And I,' wrote Gorky, 'who do not believe in God, I looked at him, I don't know why, with a great deal of circumspection and a little fear too. I looked at him and I thought: this man is like God!' But the great man wasn't able to convert Gorky to Christianity, just as Gorky was unable to convert him to Marxism. Yet both Chekhov and Gorky remained fascinated by Tolstoy.

By now, the dying Tolstoy was an object of concern to the authorities. Doctors were sent posthaste from Moscow to minister to him. Miraculously, he recovered. 'An excellent thing, a long illness: it allows one to prepare for death,' he wrote. He made the long journey back to his estate at Yasnaya Polyana, and at every station on the way, flowers, crowds and orations met him. He was to live another eight years.

Next we visited Chekhov's house-museum, where he wrote *The Three Sisters* and *The Cherry Orchard*. Chekhov, too, had an unhappy childhood, but he remained cheerful and unselfpitying all his life. His family, from Tagenrog on the Sea of Azov, was poor. His father had been a serf but had set up a shop in which his children were forced to serve. He loved music and made his children sing in the church choir. Chekhov later became an atheist, but probably for philosophical reasons. His father fled from his debts to Moscow, leaving Anton to live alone and attend school. Chekhov trained as a doctor in Moscow, but began to write early on. A letter to his brother says, 'Medicine is my legal spouse while literature is my mistress. When I get tired of one I sleep with the other.' He suffered from tuberculosis and was obliged to spend the last five years of his life in the mild climate of Yalta in the hope of recovering his health. How the sick writer wished to escape from his 'warm Siberia'.

Famous people came to see him in Yalta. Rachmaninov played the piano, which still sits in his comfortable sitting room. After many years of being a bachelor, Chekhov married a charming and talented actress from Moscow, Olga Knipper. His bad health didn't allow him to travel all the way to Moscow to see her and see her act. An exception was made, however, for his forty-fourth birthday on 17 January 1904. He was to be present for the first performance of *The Cherry Orchard*, with Olga in the principal role. The long journey was terrible.

Emaciated and exhausted, he arrived in Moscow and insisted on going to the theatre. No sooner had he taken his place than he was seized by a terrible fit of coughing. He managed to stay for the whole performance. 'I was fêted so lavishly, so warmly, and above all so unexpectedly,' he wrote, 'that I have not yet recovered from it.' He never did. In July of the same year, he died, aged forty-four.

Since we were known to have literary interests, our guide announced that a special 'literary event' had been arranged in our honour. Did we know the poems of Leyla Ukrainitsa? We were sorry that we did not, but more than happy to get to know them. We were taken to the house of the poetess in Yalta, which is now a house-museum. The curator greeted us at the door. We gathered around her in the sitting room and listened attentively as she told us the story of the poetess, first in Russian, then in English. Hers had been a 'romantic' life. She loved a man who loved another. Here, in this intimate, sad house, she had poured out poem after poem of baffled love, longing and melancholy. Eventually, she married someone else, but her husband developed tuberculosis and she nursed him devotedly. He was a musician and director of the Conservatoire of Music in Moscow. Then she herself caught the terrible disease and died of it. Ironically, her husband was to survive her by forty years. We were all moved by the details of this sad life.

The curator had something else in store for us, saying, 'We have arranged a special event in honour of your visit.' We were taken into another room, where a small group of students were waiting to perform for us. They took it in turns to read her poems, first in Russian, then in English. They were visibly nervous at performing before the 'distinguished' foreign audience. The music of romantic longing came over more soulfully in the lovely Russian sounds than in English. Next, a young girl of about twelve entered with her mother. She was to perform on the Ukrainian musical instrument, the bandura. Her mother fussed around her as she prepared to play some simple musical settings of Ukrainitsa's poems for us. She then played some Ukrainian folk songs and finished with the Ukrainian national anthem. On our behalf, I made a short speech of appreciation and gratitude to the curator. She, in her turn, thanked us profusely. The museum was about to be closed for improvements, she said. 'By your coming you have made this, our first year as a museum, a truly international one. Thank you! Thank you!'

Our journey from Yalta to Odessa was by minivan, a day-long journey in cramped conditions, but what did that matter when we would be crossing the famous steppe? Chekhov wrote a lyrical short story called *The Steppe*, based on boyhood journeys he had made in the old ox-drawn wagon train: 'You drive on for one hour, do another ... You meet upon the way a silent old barrow and a stone figure put up God knows when and by whom; a night bird floats noiselessly over the earth and little by little those legends of the Steppes, the tales of men you have met, the story of some old nurse from the Steppe and all the things you have managed to see and treasure in your soul come back to your mind ... And in the triumph, in the exuberance of happiness you are conscious of tension and yearning, as though the Steppe knew she was solitary, knew that her wealth and inspiration were wasted for the world, unsung, unwanted and through the joyful clamour one hears her mournful, hopeless call for singers, singers. It was a memorial to a landscape that was gone.'

We watched as the slender cypresses and the blue mountains gave way to the gently undulating grassy plain. Every now and again, the landscape was punctuated by swathes of dense forest, a lake, cultivated fields. We stopped several times at poorly stocked wayside cafés, where we were of immediate interest to the few men who were lounging away the day, either talking or playing chess. A fine-featured man of about fifty told us that he had been a captain in the Russian army and was now retired on a meagre pension of a few dollars a month – all foreign currency was called dollars. Sometimes he got nothing at all. He was voluble and very anxious for us to know how hard life was in Ukraine. Corruption was endemic. You could get nothing without a bribe. Did we know that policemen were not paid? They made their living from bribes. I asked about the land, agriculture. When the collective farms were done away with, the state continued to own most of the land, but farmers were given a small portion each, but neither money nor machinery to work it. As a result, the land lay neglected. The people were helpless. There was nothing they could do against vested interests.

We knew we were reaching the end of our long journey across the grassy steppe when we crossed a long, low bridge over a great span of water. It was the famous River Dnieper on its way to the Black Sea. In another forty kilometres, we were in Odessa itself.

Chekhov, Pushkin, Gogol and Herzen are all associated with this brilliant city of sun and commerce, literature and music. The violinists Ostraik and Herwitz were born here.

Unlike Kiev, Odessa is a relatively new city, only two hundred years old to Kiev's thousand. It was once a small port on the Black Sea, controlled by the Ottoman Turks. In the eighteenth century, Empress Catherine II determined to extend her Empire south to the Black Sea to counteract the power of the Turks. Catherine gave the job of opening up New Russia in the 1770s to her lover, G. Potemkin. He was spectacularly successful – he founded naval and commercial ports on the lower Dnieper and along the coast and attracted new settlers into them. Catherine, with slave labour, constructed a new port, built up the town and named it after an adjacent Greek colony called Odessos. She insisted that it should have a feminine name and had it changed to Odessa.

The man she chose to build her new city was not a Russian, but a Frenchman, the Duc de Richelieu, nephew of the more famous Cardinal de Richelieu. He was a refugee from the guillotine and was a brilliant administrator. He laid out the city on a grid system with wide boulevards and a long seafront. Foreigners were employed to build the city – Germans the gaslights, Belgians the trams, British the waterworks and Austrians the opera house. The famous Potemkin Steps from the lower city to the higher and nearly twice as broad at the bottom as at the top were built by an English architect called Upton who fled Britain while on a charge of forgery. Richelieu offered cheap land, religious toleration and exemption from military service, so many persecuted minorities flocked to the new territories from all over Europe – runaway serfs, Cossacks, Jews fleeing from persecution in Europe – who grew rich in Odessa. It is reckoned that a hundred nationalities were living in Odessa in the nineteenth century. 'It was a city of freethinkers,' said our guide. Grain from the rich hinterland rolled into the city for export to the great corn markers of Genoa, Leghorn and Marseilles.

The silent film *The Battleship Potemkin* (1925) by Eisenstein put Odessa on the world stage. The film

tells of the strike of sailors in 1905 on the battleship *Potemkin* in the Odessa harbour. There had
been years of bad harvests and there was wide-
spread unrest all over the Empire. The strike was
sparked off by the meagre and rat-infested rations
fed to the sailors. Local people, to support the
sailors, ran down the 192 steps from the upper city,
carrying food to them. As they ran, they were fired
on by tsarist troops and most were massacred.
Eisenstein's film gives a powerful visual image of
the event – he shows a stream of crimson blood
pouring down the steps as a pram with a baby adrift
in it rhythmically bounces down step after step
from top to bottom, a devastating image of cruelty.
Afterwards, there were severe reprisals and 80,000
residents out of a total of 600,000 fled.

The film was considered too provocative to be
shown – it was banned on its release in 1925 and
not shown in Europe until 1956. We looked up
from below at the famous steps to the statue of
Richelieu at the top. It was hard to imagine those
bloody scenes on this quiet, sunny morning.

The Second World War came like the god of destruction to Odessa. The Germans besieged it for
two months. It was then the home of one of the
largest and most flourishing Jewish communities in
the world. Six days after the city's capture by German and Romanian troops, a bomb exploded in
Romanian headquarters. The next day, 19,000 Jews
were burned alive. Another 16,000 were marched
to a nearby village and shot. The remaining Jews,

many of them women and children, were driven into four large warehouses and machine-gunned through holes in the walls. The rest of Odessa's Jews were sent to concentration camps where they died of disease, starvation and mass executions.

Although Odessa today is rather run-down, with broken pavements and peeling paint, it's still a lovely city. The baroque Opera House is magnificent: in it, we saw an unforgettable performance of Verdi's *Aida*. We strolled along the harbour front. There were few people about – a couple of lovers embracing on the famous steps and having their photograph taken, a babushka pushing a pram, a few townspeople – but no tourists at all. A little outdoor café with scarlet umbrellas drew us by its delicious smell of coffee. Beribboned ponies with their owners were on offer for hire, but there were no takers. An old woman tried to make a sale. A young, smartly dressed girl offered to sell us postcards. 'I am fifteen and I have been selling postcards since I was eight. I am not selling anything this morning.' A young woman passed leading a pedigree dog. I sat down on a bench beside a man, woman and small child.

'How is life here?'

'Oh, there is corruption everywhere. No, we don't have a car. On Sundays, we go to the beach. We have a barbeque with our friends. We enjoy ourselves.'

The Assumption Cathedral, with its brilliant blue and white onion domes, never fails to enchant.

It's hard to imagine that it has been completely re-built by the Soviets, for it was blown up by the Germans in 1941 in a senseless tide of destruction. Inside, the magic of Byzantine mosaics was as powerful as ever. A fashionably dressed young woman weeps continuously as she prays and blesses each icon in turn, bows low to the ground and makes the sign of the cross. Our guide tells me that she herself has no religion, as her father was a communist, but when she's inside this church, she finds peace within herself. An elderly woman sitting at a desk is receiving written petitions from the faithful. One of our group asks if she may hand in a petition. The woman abruptly refuses. Petitions must be in Russian. God, it seems, only speaks Russian.

The next day, being Sunday, we all want to attend an Orthodox service. With much difficulty, we find our way to a nearby monastery and mount a steep staircase to reach the church above. It's thronged with people – men, women, children, babes in arms all standing in utter devotion facing the Holy Doors. The people bow low, touch the floor again and again, cross themselves. The exchanges between the priest behind the Holy Doors and the cantor in the midst of the people is taking place in strict liturgical order. The rich, deep voice of the cantor is answered by the voices of the unseen choir and by the voice of the priest. Incense, vestments, colour and sound enchant the senses. A huge icon of Christ in Glory looks down from the ceiling on his devoted creatures. A priest in a magnificent mitre and vivid green vestments emerges from behind the Holy Door, now open in the iconostasis. He is accompanied by four or five pale, ascetic acolytes, also vested. He is strong and handsome with a lustrous, dark brown beard.

He begins to distribute the Eucharist to the people. He dips a large silver spoon into a silver chalice and holds it out to be received. An acolyte stands reverently by, holding out a red cloth between the chalice and the receiver in case a drop of the holy substance should be accidentally spilled. Arms crossed, mouth reverently opened, the wine is received, sign of the cross made, the chalice kissed. Even a baby of a few months is held out to receive a little wine. Some of us line up with those waiting to receive. A woman starts forward from a group who are standing to one side. She whispers to us, 'No breakfast! No lipstick!' They are from Bratislava and have been refused for these reasons. We fall out of line at this news. The faithful, having received, turn towards another vested acolyte who offers them a cube of bread from a silver salver. I go up to him. *'Mozna?'* (May I?)

*'Ne Mozna,'* he replies, but people beckon to us, recognising our difficulty. They point to a table at the side where bread and wine that have not been consecrated stand waiting. We eat – it is a sign of hospitality. It's very moving to be with these ordinary Ukrainian people here in this holy place.

❧

Odessa is full of museums of every kind. We went straight to the writers' museum. It's housed in a handsome building with exhibits of manuscripts, photos and memorabilia imaginatively set out. Two fine-looking elderly ladies, one with a profile Picasso might have painted, do the honours. They react enthusiastically to our interest. 'From Belfast! How interesting! We have not had any Irish people before.' They scarcely see tourists, though some come from tourist ships anchored in the harbour and an occasional German or Italian. Yes, we had heard of Pushkin, Gogol, Chekhov, Tolstoy. They tell us about them – they are very proud of their writers. A middle-aged Englishman is the only other tourist present, though he's busy loudly showing how he can read the letters of the Cyrillic alphabet. We thank these devoted women who tend the sacred flame. We are glad to have come.

On the way back to the hotel, we come upon a new building, doors open, lights within. We look in, curious. It's a new mosque. Two men come forward and beckon us to come inside. They motion us to take off our shoes and drape us in long black gowns with hoods trimmed with gold. A young girl, head covered, comes forward and takes us in charge. She is studying Arabic culture at the university but is not herself a Muslim. She explains the layout of the mosque and its purpose – the huge, empty prayer hall, richly carpeted with its low mihrab indicating the direction of Mecca, is strikingly the opposite of what we have just seen in the

Orthodox church, with its sensuous beauty of sight, sound and smell. Yet the mosque holds the spirit too. The two places of worship are a reminder of the multicultural Odessa, now reasserting itself after the years of Soviet atheism.

As Anne and I wander along the seafront, we come upon an art museum with a small sign saying 'icons for sale'. As we had nothing of this order to buy in Ukraine, we go inside. Two young women come forward, very anxious to make a sale for foreign currency. There are only five or six icons for sale. I bought a beautiful Madonna and Child which, we were told, had been painted by a Bulgarian woman who had won prizes for her work. It's unusual for an icon painter to be a woman. Anne bought one too. The women had no means of dealing in credit cards, and we didn't have enough money. We were about to leave Odessa in thirty minutes' time! We were at a sad impasse. Could we borrow the money from our friends? They were back in the hotel and we only had fifteen or twenty minutes to get back and do the deal. The two women immediately shut up shop and raced with us back to the hotel, icons under their arms. The group was waiting, suitcases ready. We quickly borrowed enough money, the icons were handed over and the women smiled and disappeared, satisfied. This Odessa Madonna and Child icon now hangs on my bedroom wall.

At the airport, waiting to be called to our flight to Kiev, I chat with Tanya and Olga, our guides, and thank them for looking after us so well.

'It's a pity you don't have more tourists. Your country is extremely interesting,' I say.

'It is difficult to attract tourists. When we were part of the USSR, they looked after tourism. We were on the main itineraries from Moscow and St Petersburg. Now we are on our own and we have no resources. But we are thinking of something which may prove very profitable. You know that hundreds of thousands of German soldiers were killed here in Ukraine? No one knows where they are buried. It is not yet possible for Germans to mourn their war dead in any public fashion as we mourn ours. We in the tourist trade are making desperate efforts to trace the German graves, to find where they are buried. There are people who know but they will not speak. We are searching the cemeteries. Irina is at this moment doing just that!'

Incredulous, I ask, 'But do you really feel so much for your recent cruel enemy that you want to honour their graves?'

'Oh, no! It is not that at all! We have absolutely no wish to honour their graves, but if we can find the graves, we will tell the German relations who will come to visit them. That will bring hundreds if not thousands of people to our agency!'

The ironies of fate are never ending.